FRUITLOOPS & DIPSTICKS

FRUITLOOPS & DIPSTICKS

ULF STARK

GECKO PRESS

English edition first published in 2010 by Gecko Press
PO Box 9335, Marion Square, Wellington 6141, New Zealand
info@geckopress.com

First published by Bonnier Carlsen Bokförlag, Stockholm, Sweden
Published in the English language by arrangement with Bonnier Group Agency, Stockholm, Sweden

Gecko Press gratefully acknowledges the support of the Swedish Arts Council and the Baltic Centre for Writers and Translators.

A catalogue record for this book is available from the National Library of New Zealand.

Cover illustration by Harriet Bailey
Design by Spencer Levine, Wellington, New Zealand
Printed by Everbest, China

ISBN paperback 978-1-877467-58-5

For more curiously good books, visit www.geckopress.com

**There are no lies,
only half-truths**

Spinoza

first chapter

I celebrate my birthday, the house has its final hurrah, we move and leave something behind

The house was quiet. The first rays of sunlight filtered between the buildings in the square, shimmering on my face. Even though it was far too early, I got up. I couldn't go back to sleep anyway.

It was the morning of my twelfth birthday, the day everything started.

Our apartment looked like the rubbish heap we were about to move to. There were piles of things everywhere – sheets, curtains, old clothes, the silly ornaments Mum collected, books, drawing pads and paint brushes, old magazines. I picked my way through the mess.

I poked my nose into the sitting room.

Mum was peacefully asleep, covered in an old silver fox fur because she was always so cold at night. Our dog, Kilroy, lay at her feet. As I stood in the doorway, he blinked at me sleepily, surprised to see me awake before he was. Then he slid down from the bed and assaulted me with small grunts, panting and slobbering.

'Shh! You'll wake Mum!' I whispered in his furry ear.

We went out to the kitchen. I found a plastic bowl and a whisk among the heaps of pots, paper-wrapped glasses, plates, sauce jugs, soup bowls and place mats. I whisked the cream and smoothed it over the cake I'd made the night before while Mum was busy finishing off an illustration for a magazine. I topped it off with twelve sparklers left over from Guy Fawkes, because I couldn't find any birthday candles.

'Sod it,' I said.

Kilroy licked the cream from my fingers and looked at me with sorrowful eyes, as if he understood how terrible everything had become and that things were going to get even more complicated. I bent down and buried my face in his creamy, soft fur and wished I could disappear in there, too, like being inside a white cloud.

I didn't want a birthday.

I didn't want to leave everything behind. I didn't want to leave this boring apartment where I was so happy, or the grumpy old sourpuss Mrs Rapp on the ground floor who always complained that Mum played the saxophone at night and that Kilroy peed outside the front door. I didn't want to leave my friends or my school or the café in the square. We were moving to a draughty little house south of town. As far as I was concerned we might as well move to some old hole in the country with dribbling cows and fat babies. It would take two hours to get back here by train. But the worst thing was that we were going to share the house with Ingvar, an idiot Mum had decided to move in with. If love could trick people into doing stupid things like that, I would never fall in love!

I sat for a moment at the kitchen window, thinking about all the things I didn't want to do. When the kitchen clock chimed eight I set a tray with the cake, a can of

Fanta, a coffee cup, a dusty plastic flower I found in the sitting room, and a bowl of dog food. The clock was huge, made from mahogany and brass, and it clanged like a mad thing. Mum inherited it from Grandpa, along with a whole lot more clocks, when he moved into the old people's home. They all pinged, donged and dinged in different places and at different times, because Mum never bothered to set them. But the kitchen clock was always right. I set it myself so I would know when it was time to leave for school.

'Let's go,' I said to Kilroy.

I knew Mum would forget my birthday. She never remembered that sort of thing. And when it came to name days it didn't matter anyway. My name is Simone, and that horrible name doesn't have a day of its own, luckily.

I lit the sparklers and marched into the sitting room. Kilroy smooched against my legs and woofed happily, as I sang, 'Happy birthday to me, happy birthday to me!' and the sparklers spluttered and sparked.

We didn't sound very good and Mum turned to face the wall.

I put the crackling firework cake on a chair beside the bed and shook Mum awake.

'What is it?' she grunted from under the fur. 'Can't you be a bit more quiet?'

'I'm celebrating my birthday,' I said. 'There's cake if you want some!'

She blinked herself awake and smiled dazzlingly at me and the sparklers and at Kilroy. Then she stumbled out of bed and hugged me tight. Her plump body smelled of perfume and old tobacco.

'Darling! Fancy forgetting!' she said. 'Are you mad at me? Everything's been so topsy-turvy lately. Now, let's see about your birthday present!'

She pulled on the fur coat and pattered among the ruins to see if she could find a suitable present, poking her red-lacquered toenails here and there at the piles she had started to sort on the floor. She dug through boxes and then stopped in front of the big gilt-framed mirror. She pushed her fingers through her black-dyed hair. In the fur, she looked like the lady-star of a big Russian film. Dust swirled around her like a snow storm in the Siberian tundra.

'It's not necessary,' I said.

'What?' she said.

'I don't need a present,' I said.

'Don't need a present!' she repeated in an injured voice, looking at me accusingly in the mirror. 'You're just saying that to make me feel bad, you little roach!'

I was a pale shadow behind her in the mirror. I looked like one of those little rumpled ghost animals that live in the artificial moonlit night-room at the zoo. I almost disappeared in the light from Mum.

'Okay,' I said. 'Of course I want a present.'

Mum rummaged in a wooden trunk we'd brought down from the attic the day before, fishing out a dusty glass ball that she rubbed against the fur till it shone like a lamp in the wan morning light creeping in through the kitchen doorway.

'This is for you,' she said. 'It's a crystal ball. Once upon a time it belonged to your great-grandmother. Lord knows what it has foreseen in its time, good and bad. Maybe you will see your true love in it?'

When I took it the glass ball felt cold. It was so heavy I almost dropped it on my toes.

'Is this where you found Ingvar?' I said. 'In that case I wouldn't give much for it.'

Mum pretended not to hear. She sat on the edge of the mahogany monster, the bed that would be mine when we moved. She ate cake, fed Kilroy and teased me till I almost forgot what a horrible day it was.

'We'll stick together, you and me,' she said.

Then she got up to make a lot of calls to all the other people who lived in the building, and she unpacked the plates she had already packed and started to knead an enormous, porous dough. She was planning an afternoon party. She loved parties. A farewell party was also practical because it meant you could get rid of a whole lot of things you didn't want to take with you.

I picked up the rest of the birthday cake and went out with Kilroy.

At around four o'clock, people started to pour in. By then we had most things out of the way, piled up in boxes around the walls. First to come was the Twig who has a morning newspaper run and usually arrives early. She smiled magnificently with her false teeth, and looked around nosily. Then the others came in dribs and drabs, all the names from the signs on the doors: Mr Joholainen, the Nystedts with their quarrelsome small children, the Engmans, Mr Riklund, the Vikmans, old Gustafsson and Mrs Rapp. They all carried dishes and plates of sausages and cheese, pickled cucumbers and herrings, spiced plums, pirogues and chops. Mrs Rapp, the old goat, had a piece of sour blood pudding wrapped in greaseproof paper. She looked crossly at everyone.

Mum loved being in her stilettos and an elephant-sized hat which tinkled with the thousand glass beads that dangled like a veil from its brim. I felt left out. I thought it was all so pointless. What was the point of getting to know all these people we had never met, just when we were about to leave?

After a while the men from the moving company arrived to collect our things. Mum kept giving them food. People were constantly going off to get more to eat and drink from the different apartments. The voices got louder and louder and smoke from the cigarettes and cigars made a cloud up near the ceiling.

Mr Joholainen got his accordion and Mum joined in with her saxophone. I curled up on some boxes, and watched the dancers strutting around. Mrs Rapp closed her eyes as she danced with the muscular Mr Riklund. One of the moving men was twirling around with Mrs Engman. The Nystedt's five-year-old sat in the middle of the floor, trying to feed Kilroy from a tin of cold fish balls.

In the middle of all this, the phone rang. It was Ingvar.

'Can I talk to your mother?' he said, when I answered.

'She's not home,' I said.

'I know she's there,' he said. 'Why haven't you left yet?'

'Mum has,' I said.

'I know she's there,' he sighed. 'But okay. See you tomorrow morning.'

'Who was that?' called Mum.

'Just some idiot who got the wrong number,' I said, smiling.

Mr Vikman, determinedly crossing the floor, slipped on the fish balls and stood on Kilroy's tail. Kilroy disappeared out the kitchen door with a howl. It was too much for him, first being force-fed doughy fish balls and then having his tail squashed. I'd had enough too. After a while I dozed off on top of my boxes.

I don't know what time it was when Mum woke me.

'We're going now,' she said.

'Okay,' I said.

No one at the party noticed when we disappeared.

'It's almost a shame to leave now,' said Mum in the doorway.

'Mmm,' I said, which didn't mean anything.

The chandelier swayed slowly in the draught from an open window. Light glimmered on the wallpaper which had dark patches where paintings and things had been taken down. The moon shone like an omniscient eye watching the theatre inside, the dancers billowing among the remaining pieces of furniture, the table covered in empty plates, empty glasses and smouldering cigarette butts.

We packed ourselves in with the rest of the load. I rested my head on Mum's knee.

'I feel like we've left something behind,' she said, stroking my forehead.

I didn't answer. I wasn't worried. She always forgot things. And anyway, we'd left a whole lot of things behind on purpose. I dozed off again to the hum of the engine and didn't see any of the bridges and roads we drove over, not even the thousands of lights that Stockholm decorates its own birthday cake with every night.

second chapter

We discover what we left behind, we look for what has disappeared and I think about what it means to have a mother like mine

The sun poured in through the windows which still had no curtains but were shrouded with dust and ingrained dirt. The light pricked my eyes. I woke to the sound of snuffling and whimpering.

It was Mum.

She was spread out on a mattress on a platform of boxes. One leg, clad in a shiny stocking, stuck out over the edge. I was wrapped in a pile of blankets.

Something wasn't right!

This was definitely not the proper way to wake up; not to a whimpering mother, on a strange floor with the sun in my eyes. Normally I got woken by a cold, wet nose pushing into my stomach or poking me in my armpit or ear. It was a beautiful way to wake up.

I sat up and listened.

Outside, gulls shrieked, together with thrushes. Inside the boxes you could hear the clocks tick-ticking. But there was no lovely sound of paws on a cork floor or the peaceful tugging of dog teeth on shoe leather, or the snuffling, panting sound Kilroy made when he was asleep.

I immediately realized what we'd forgotten.

Kilroy!

How can you forget your own dog?

I was furious. It was so impossible and so unnatural.

At least, I should say that for Mum it was the most natural thing in the world. I should be thankful she hadn't forgotten me.

Although I knew there was no point, I searched the house. I even listened to see if a strange doglike sound was coming from any of the boxes. But apart from a lot of ticking and clanging, there was nothing.

I got crosser and crosser the more I looked, because I knew that it was hopeless. I searched through what was called the sitting room, I looked in the kitchen, and I stamped up the rickety stairs. There were two rooms up there. One was going to be mine. It had a view of the lake and the rubbish dump. The other one was Mum and Ingvar's room.

Ingvar was, as I've said, Mum's new boyfriend. You'd think she'd picked him up somewhere they sold stupid, boring people cheap. He wore ties and small hats so you couldn't see that he was almost bald.

Everything was hopeless! First we had to leave Linda and Ulrika and my other friends and move to a falling-down old house in the middle of nowhere. Then I had to live with a hat-idiot. And on top of everything, never see Kilroy again! It was too much.

I roared down the stairs so fast the stairs bowed in the middle, flew into the kitchen and swept some plates off the shelf. That should have woken anybody up. Mum continued to sleep, unmoved. Now she made a sound like a tiger, a muffled gurgling sound in her throat. She smiled in her sleep. I couldn't cope with her smiling as well.

I grabbed hold of something in a bag and threw it at her. It was a half-full bag of flour. It exploded on her head and spread a white cloud around her.

'Why can't you be like other mothers?' I screamed.

'Hello?' someone said from the middle of the cloud. 'Who's there?'

'Why can't you be absolutely normal?' I yelled.

'Is that you my sweet poppet?' coughed my mother. 'Don't you feel well?'

'Why do you always have to forget everything?' I cried.

My eyes were filled with tears. I grabbed a box of macaroni and threw it at her.

'Are you completely mad?' she yelled. 'What's the matter with you?'

'You're the one who's mad!' I shouted.

I heaved the iron at her. But now Mum was ready and she caught it mid-air.

'Stop it, Simone!' she said. 'It's not funny anymore.'

But I wasn't going to stop. I got hold of a box filled with shoes and tubes of toothpaste and soap and I tipped it over her. I threw things and sniffed.

'Calm down!' she shouted. 'What do you want?'

'I want a normal, everyday mother,' I snuffled. 'Not one who forgets everything.'

She got up out of bed. She held my arms. We lay on the floor and my body shook with crying. Mum was completely covered in flour and a shoe had caught her on the lip so she was bleeding.

She looked at me unhappily.

'What have I forgotten?' she asked.

'Nothing special,' I said, and I couldn't help sounding bitter. 'Just our dog.'

'Kilroy,' Mum sighed. 'I knew we'd forgotten something.'

'I don't want to lose Kilroy,' I hiccupped.

'Darling. We'll find him, you'll see,' she said, stroking my wet cheeks with her big hand. 'It will be all right, dear.'

But her voice sounded sad, as if she didn't believe it herself. Just then Ingvar appeared carrying two suitcases, wearing his fusspot hat on the back of his neck.

'You two look cheerful,' he said.

We borrowed Ingvar's car to see if Kilroy had stayed close to the apartment. It was a little yellow Fiat that Mum could drive really fast. Ingvar was a real nana on the road. He'd drive so slowly that Mum couldn't cope and she'd bounce up and down in her seat. Ingvar, on the other hand, got very scared and felt sick whenever Mum drove. So Ingvar stayed at home.

'Drive carefully,' he said as we drove off.

'We'll probably not make more than one or two small dings,' I said.

It was Sunday and the sun was pelting down and all the leaves on the trees were about to burst open, cheered on by finches and gulls and thrushes. And the roads were full of cars on their way to every possible place.

'People drive so slowly it's not funny,' said Mum, swinging left and right so that I swayed from side to side in the back seat. 'It's not surprising they go to sleep at the wheel and drive into poles and things.'

Suddenly we were outside our old building which in a funny kind of way already felt foreign. Mrs Engman was outside the door. She had one of our old mats rolled up under one arm. She looked very embarrassed and didn't know what to do with it.

'I was going to give it a shake,' she said.

'Why don't you keep that old thing, dear Mrs Engman,' said Mum. 'That was the idea.'

'Well, in that case, I can only say thank you,' she said.

'Have you seen Kilroy?' I asked.

She hadn't. And he wasn't in the apartment. It still had a heavy atmosphere of after-party muddle. The floor was sticky with food. A rickety Karl Johan chair leaned against the wall. Otherwise the apartment was quite empty of furniture. Mum hooked down the chandelier and hung it like a rucksack over her shoulders.

'We may as well take this with us,' she said. 'If no one else wants it.'

On the way home I sat with the chandelier. It tinkled as we turned corners. Otherwise the car was quiet. We were so upset we didn't want to talk about anything. Mum tried to drive slowly, so I could see if Kilroy was walking along the road.

But he wasn't.

We took big detours, criss-crossing through town. It was as if neither of us wanted to go home to a house full of moving boxes. We stopped at all the parks to see if he was there. He might have found a place where there were other dogs, Mum thought, where he wouldn't feel so lonely.

At the last park there were a lot of dogs – big, dribbling beasts and ones that looked like long-haired guinea pigs. Mum and I went looking in different directions.

When I came back, a small crowd of people had gathered around Mum. She was standing there, tugging at a white Swedish Lappdog which looked a bit like Kilroy. On the other side was a man in a green hunting coat. He had a long face, fire-engine red under his cap.

'Let go of my dog, you cross-eyed pig snout!' screamed Mum, staring at the man with her wild yellow eyes.

The man took a step backwards. He was actually a little cross-eyed. His face got a bit redder.

'That really does it,' he said. 'Would you please leave my dog alone and take yourself away from here. Otherwise I can't answer for the consequences.'

'Are you threatening me, you fat bag of jelly?' hissed Mum. 'First you steal my dog and then you threaten an innocent women. Is this your normal Sunday pleasure, eh?'

Mum can be very harsh when she wants to be. Now she was getting really worked up. In her defence, she truly did believe it was Kilroy. She's not much good at recognizing dogs. Or people either, for that matter.

'This is extraordinary,' spluttered the man, and his eyes travelled around beneath his cap like balls in a game of pinball. 'Is this supposed to be some kind of joke?'

'Only you can answer that,' spat Mum. 'I'm getting tired of this, old man. Now shove off and let go of the dog.'

The man did let go of the dog, but only to pinch himself in the face with his sausage-like fingers. He wanted to see if he was awake or if it was just a bad dream.

He took a couple of steps towards Mum. He was so upset he was shaking and his long green coat quivered around his chunky walking boots.

'I'll show you whose dog this is,' he puffed, wringing his hands.

There's going to be a fight, I thought. But just then a couple of big guys in tracksuits grabbed hold of the man's arms.

'Just you cool down a bit,' said one of them. 'You've done enough damage as it is.'

'What strange types of people there are in this world,' sighed Mum.

She looked like a flaming goddess in the red evening dress she'd grabbed as we rushed out the door. The soft material billowed in the wind, like wings on a furious angel. Her yellow eyes sparked and her black hair swayed like a wimple.

'Come on, Kilroy, let's go,' she said, walking through the ring of observers.

The strange dog followed obediently. It wagged its tail and licked Mum's fingers happily. No one could doubt that it was her dog.

'Goliath! Goliath!' shrieked the man.

But the dog didn't even turn its head. It seemed pleased to get away from the angry man and the snooty name Goliath.

'Darling, there you are!' said Mum when she noticed me at last. 'Look who I've found!'

She pointed proudly at the white dog gliding beside her with its nose in the air.

'Come! Quick!' I half whispered, half shouted, pulling on her arm. 'That's not Kilroy!'

'What?'

'That's not Kilroy,' I said. 'Can't you tell? It's another dog. Hurry up, let's get to the car!'

'But what shall I do with it? I'll have to give it back. Oh my Lord!'

I made her understand that it wasn't such a good idea to go back with the poor dog just at that minute. We half ran over the grass. When we were getting into the car the dog tried to get into the back seat. We bribed it with half a packet of Rollos to stay outside.

Through the back window I could see it loping back to the dwindling crowd of people.

On the way home in the car we had to laugh about Mum and the man and the dog that had followed her so happily. For a moment it almost felt good again. But then our laughter dried up. When we got home we had no appetite, even though Ingvar had made soup. We didn't even find it funny when Ingvar's tie dropped in the soup as he was serving up.

Mum felt ridiculous, stupid and a complete failure.

'You're right,' she muttered over her soup bowl. 'I should be more like a proper mother. I'll have to take a little more responsibility for the home.'

She made an effort to be a proper mother for the whole evening.

She went over the floor with a shiny monster of a vacuum cleaner which drowned out anyone trying to speak. She dusted and mopped and rubbed the windows till they squeaked. She whisked away spider webs and made piles of dirty washing. She unpacked boxes and moved furniture around. She watered the flowers and made tea and was impossible to talk to.

'Don't think I'm doing this because I think it's fun,' she said every now and again. And her voice sounded complaining and sacrificing and angry all at the same time, like a proper mother's.

When darkness fell on the newly washed floors she asked Ingvar to hang the chandelier from the ceiling. But as soon as he climbed onto a rickety stool with the chandelier in his arms, he went yellow-green in the face and his knees started to quiver and wobble. The chandelier tinkled again like a thousand small bells and the stool danced over the floor with small clacking steps.

'What are you doing?' asked Mum, staring at Ingvar in consternation.

I was speechless. I had no idea that the boring old fart was a trapeze artist.

'Help me down! Help me down!' he begged as the stool continued past a brass sideboard and out towards the hall.

Just before the stool reached the threshold, which I was wondering how he would negotiate, Mum lifted down Ingvar and the chandelier. His legs were still shaking and his face was dripping with sweat.

'Darling, what's the matter?' Mum asked, sounding normal again.

'It's nothing,' squeaked Ingvar. 'It will pass in a minute. It's just that I'm a little bit afraid of heights, that's all. Actually, I'm very prone to fainting.'

He collapsed in a chair at the kitchen table and Mum bathed his balding scalp with a linen napkin dipped in water. She had forgotten she was trying to be an ordinary mother. And I thought that I would probably rather have her as she was. Most of the time, anyway.

I stared thoughtfully at the crystal ball I'd been given as a birthday present. Somehow it had ended up on the kitchen table. Suddenly it glowed from the inside. A red speck grew and soon the whole ball was glowing like a snow globe.

Shining inside was a blue square that I saw evolve, stretch out and become a door with glass panes, a door handle and everything! It looked exactly like our own new front door, even though it was only a few centimetres high.

Then the door handle turned and the door opened. In the gap I could see the garden path for a moment, with daffodils, Easter lilies and pearl hyacinths either side, and fruit trees in the distance. I saw a shadow move over the gravel path by the cherry tree.

I held my breath as if the picture inside was a light that would be snuffed out by the smallest breeze. And then the door and the light and everything disappeared as quickly as it had come!

What did it mean? What had I seen?

'Imagination,' said Ingvar when I told him and Mum what I'd seen in the glass ball. 'If you stare at the same point long and hard enough you can be almost hypnotized by it. It creates pictures inside your head, a bit like when you dream. Do you understand?'

Ingvar loved to explain things. Mum and I never listened to his long, drawn-out spiels. But it didn't matter to Ingvar. He didn't notice.

'Darling,' said Mum. 'What you saw means that soon we'll have a visitor.'

'Don't fill the girl's mind with that sort of superstitious rubbish,' said Ingvar, holding his knees which were still trying to hop.

But I knew who was coming.

Kilroy.

third chapter

We have a visitor, the clocks are set and we learn something sad

At six o'clock the next morning there was a knock at the door, so hard the glass shook in its panes.

'Someone's knocking!' screamed Ingvar.

His voice echoed from the toilet. He sat locked in there every morning, groaning and moaning about his constipation. Every evening he ate a huge pile of prunes and raisins to help things along. It didn't.

'Can't you hear that knocking?' he puffed.

We could hear it. The heavy blows continued downstairs.

It had to be Kilroy. Someone had found him! Maybe he was injured or sick. That's why they were banging so hard.

I rushed down the stairs. Mum was already halfway there even though she was normally very slow in the mornings. In a single movement, she threw herself at the door and opened it. We both expected to see Kilroy on the step with his intense eyes and wagging tail. We looked down.

But there was no Kilroy.

Instead, there was a pair of black high-heeled boots. Above them was a pair of baggy, white long johns, flapping in the morning breeze, beneath a chalk-white hospital nightshirt nipped in at the waist with a length of red rubber hose. Around the neck, a shining gold pocket watch dangled on a thick gold chain.

There stood a gangly man in his eighties with a completely bald head and a big, white, droopy moustache. His slightly upturned eyes shone clear blue and alert, and he snorted happily through the strands of hair in his nostrils. He looked very stately.

'Olga!' he cried.

'Father!' said Mum.

It was Grandpa.

He took Mum's face in his huge hands and kissed her on both cheeks with a noisy smack. Tears ran in streams down his thin cheeks, wetting his moustache.

Then he grabbed me round the waist and lifted me up to his face. His mouth smelled of onions and earth. He shook his head slowly, looking at me as if he could see right inside me. His eyes were so full of sympathy that I shuddered. What could he see in there?

'Poor little thing,' he said softly, and put me carefully back on the floor and kissed me on my forehead.

'What are you doing here, Father?' Mum cried when the first moment of surprise had passed.

'I'm here to stay, my girl. But help me off now with these terrible death traps.'

He shakily lifted a foot and waved one of the high-heeled leather boots. How he had managed to walk in them at all was a mystery.

'Where in heaven's name did you get hold of those?'

'At the hospital, my little chicken. The staff cloakroom. They belong to the charge nurse. They were the only ones that fit.'

The boots were stuck as if they were glued on. Mum and I helped pull. With quiet 'plops' they were detached from his feet. At the same time, a number of clocks started chiming syncopated chimes.

Grandpa shuddered and held his gold watch up to his nose.

'Have you not set the clocks, you silly woman?' he rumbled.

In bare feet he tramped through the house and set every clock to the right time and wound up the ones that were quiet and still.

He went from room to room.

When he opened the door to the toilet he found Ingvar sitting there sweating, red-blue in the face.

'And what sort of sly fox would you be?' said Grandpa.

Ingvar stood up in terror and shuffled forwards with his trousers and undies around his ankles.

He stretched out his hand to introduce himself.

'My name is Ingvar Laurin,' he said politely, searching for Grandpa's hand.

Grandpa took a step back and giggled noisily while he observed Ingvar from top to toe.

'What have you got on? You should change into something more substantial.'

Grandpa turned on his heel and left Ingvar who, with ears flaming, saw the white-dressed figure disappear, his long johns and nightshirt swaying around his legs.

Grandpa had sat himself down in the heavy oak rocking chair with carved lion heads on its back. He rocked slowly, smoking one of Mum's black cigarettes. There were cups of steaming tea and a plate of biscuits, untouched.

'I've come here to die,' he said. 'That's why I've come.'

The room was completely silent, as if even the clocks held their breath for a moment. Grandpa stroked his moustache. He looked exhausted. Only his eyes shone clear blue, like a summer sky beneath the white clouds of his eyebrows.

Ingvar wriggled as if he wanted to say something. But Grandpa waved him away with his hand.

'I know, I know!' he said, irritated. 'It might be inconvenient. But at that terrible hospital they won't let you die in peace. You don't have time to die, with all the blood tests and thermometers they stick into you and sheets that need changing and pills to be swallowed and the devil and his grandmother!'

Then he quietened down again. The rocking chair that for a moment had tilted worryingly returned to its earlier rocking rhythm.

'Otherwise it wasn't so bad. I can't complain. Very sweet old ladies and old men, nutritious but boring food, wonderful nurses, a witch or two, and a beautiful orchestra. But it wasn't a good place to die in. That's just the way it is.'

Mum looked at him.

'I knew it,' she said. 'I knew that soon I would see my father in the doorway. Dear Father! I'm so happy you came.'

Mum smiled at him. I saw she was trying not to cry.

Grandpa smiled back.

I smiled too because I could feel that sorrow was on its way, huge and bitter. But still everything was so unreal.

Ingvar smiled too, because everyone else was smiling.

Grandpa took a little slurp of tea as if he was swallowing all these smiles. Then he started to cough, a cough that boomed like an avalanche in his chest and made him throw himself forwards.

'What sort of tea is this?' he croaked when the worst was over. 'Teabag tea! How can anyone drink anything so disgusting? Dishwater and wrung-out rags! Are you trying to kill me?'

Ingvar, who had made the tea, squirmed.

'Wouldn't it still be best … I mean, shouldn't we ring the hospital?' he began.

'Quiet now, Ingvar, please,' said Mum, placing her hand on his arm.

'Who's that clown?' said Grandpa, nodding at Ingvar. 'What's he doing here?'

'That's just someone I am in love with,' said Mum. 'Why, I'm not sure.'

Grandpa gave a tired sigh.

'Oh well,' he said. 'Never mind, sometimes that's the way it is. But I'm all done in now. I've been out walking all morning. And I can't walk any more. I need to lie down. I'll take Simone's room for the time being.'

And he disappeared up the stairs.

'Don't forget to return the boots!' he called down.

The moon shone in through the bare windowpanes. It was blowing outside, and branches and bushes cast uneasy shadows on the walls. I stuck my head into my pillow and bit hard, hard into the white cloth.

'I don't want it!' I screamed into the pillow. 'Do you hear me, God? You mustn't do it!'

That day I didn't go to my new school as I was supposed to. We went to the hospital. They couldn't believe Grandpa had managed to walk all the way to our house. When he was there, he could hardly manage to get from the bed to the toilet. His legs didn't hold him up any more, they said. They wanted us to bring Grandpa back again immediately. Ingvar thought we should, too. It was better for Grandpa to be in a place where there were resources to look after him, he said. For his own sake. To say nothing of the fact that he had reached the stage known as senility. That was something Ingvar and the hospital both agreed on. But Mum didn't say anything. She just picked up his things. There wasn't much.

In the other corner of the room was a fat little old man with gentle eyes, eating bananas and pretending he couldn't hear what was being said. But when we were ready to go he waved me over to him.

'Say hello to Ivan,' he said. 'Tell him we'll miss him in the orchestra. It will be empty without his cello and his funny little tantrums.

'God knows who will take his place now,' he said, looking dejected.

'You can choose,' said Mum in the car, driving faster and more wildly than usual, out of sheer nastiness towards Ingvar who sat in the back seat with terror in his eyes. 'Either you move out or you accept that Father will live with us.'

I hoped he would move out.

A shooting star fell crookedly right in front of the window, reminding me of how Grandpa and I used to look at the night sky through his telescope every summer on the island. I wished silently that he would never die.

Grandpa had always been there. He had shown me flowers and birds and given them names. 'Your name is fir, your name is blowfly, you nasty thing! And you, you little scallywag, your name is wagtail!'

Then he poked at them with his walking stick as if he were the Godfather himself. He taught me how to swim and wrestle. He taught me to read and swear. He didn't mean to teach me swearing. I learned by listening to his regular outbursts.

'Where did she get that word from?' he said the first time he heard me.

'She learned it from you, my darling man,' said Grandma, back when she was alive.

'By hell no!' he protested. Then he realized what he'd said and laughed hilariously. He was really very proud of his role as the Godfather. He was my father because I didn't know any other; and God, that was a role he took on anyway.

But now I prayed to another God, who I wasn't even sure existed, that Grandpa would live.

'Take Ingvar instead!' I begged, feeling really bad and nasty.

'Please God, take the hat idiot instead!'

Then I fell asleep and I dreamt that Grandpa was gliding over the water in his rocking chair. He sat quietly puffing on a cigar while the rocking chair rocked over the waves, giving way to plastic sailboats and windsurfers and then slowly steering out towards the horizon. His gold watch cast reflections from the sun, shining like a little star.

I woke up because someone was gently pulling my ear lobe.

'Hello, my little dove,' he whispered. 'How are you?'

'Bad,' I said, starting to cry.

And he rubbed his big nose against mine just like he did when I was little. His moustache tickled and he smelt like earth. And just like before, when he was a good and wise God and I was just a little whippersnapper whom he happened to love, I told him everything – about having to move and Kilroy and Ingvar and Mum and how I couldn't cope if he wasn't there. And when I cried I could feel the hard lump of anger inside me, beating like a heart. Why was all this happening to me? Why did all these stupid, sad things have to happen at the same time?

'Poor little thing,' said Grandpa. 'We're a family of eccentrics and bores, what we call fruitloops and dipsticks. Your mother is a fruitloop, like me. My mother was also a fruitloop. And I know they're not easy to live with. Then there are a whole lot of dipsticks. They're maybe a little easier to get along with. But damn it – they're not much fun!'

'Am I a fruitloop?' I asked, trying to smile.

'You'll probably turn into one,' said Grandpa.

He patted me slowly and thoughtfully on my neck,

where my short hair became curly and went in all directions.

'We're all filled with forces we don't know about,' Grandpa went on. 'Like the sea, which is full of fish and algae and currents and life and all kinds of strange things. The dipsticks carefully build thin, ugly bridges over these unknown waters. They're afraid of getting wet in case they ruin their shoes. We fruitloops like to crawl around down there. We put ourselves in the path of the currents and let them carry us along. Even though it's risky. And even though the dipsticks look at us with fear and disdain.'

I didn't really understand what he meant. His hand felt safe and reassuring on my neck. Still tears continued to fall. They felt cold, as if they came from the beating lump in my chest.

'Be careful of the bad winds,' whispered Grandpa in my ear before he hobbled out into the dark and disappeared up the stairs.

What did he mean by that? Was he a bit crazy after all?

I couldn't cope with all the fruitloops and dipsticks and hat idiot fusspots inhabiting this house.

Just then the window flew open on its hinge, caught by a strong gust of wind. It swept with it a pair of flowerpots on the windowsill and a pile of bills Mum had sorted the night before, and forced its way into my heart.

I could feel I was being filled up with ill will and nastiness.

fourth chapter

I begin my new school, my name betrays me and I make the acquaintance of loser Isaac

Mum came into the kitchen where I sat trying to eat some pieces of toast I had burnt black, purely out of bad temper. She was wearing a leopard-print dress which showed most of her legs and breasts. To complete her outfit she had chosen a pair of fire-engine red boots, black fishnet stockings and a pair of fantastic sunglasses speckled with small sparkly stars.

'Are you up already?' she said. 'I thought I'd come with you to school.'

'I thought you were going to a masquerade ball,' I said as crossly and hurtfully as I could.

'Won't that be nice?' Mum said, as if she hadn't heard me. 'Then I can say hello to your teacher and see your friends.'

'They aren't my friends. I haven't met them yet.'

'What's the matter with you?' she said, upset. 'I thought you said you wanted a proper mother. A proper mother would surely go with her daughter on her first day at her new school.'

'A proper mother wouldn't look like that.'

'Like what?' she said, taking off her sunglasses so she could see me better. 'What's wrong with my clothes?'

'You look like a crazy jungle woman from a Tarzan film,' I said, and I could tell that the evil was starting to make itself at home in my heart.

Ingvar came stumbling in from the toilet, sat down at the table and piled a heap of wheatgrass and yeast and ground nuts into his yoghurt.

'What's all this about?' he crackled between crumbs of high-fibre crispbread.

'My daughter doesn't want me to go with her to school. She thinks I look like some sort of wild creature.'

'Of course your mother should go with you,' he said, chewing the twenty-four times you are supposed to for every mouthful.

'Never!' I hissed and got up to go.

On my way out I swept aside a carton of low-fat milk with a movement which might not have been on purpose. A blue-white waterfall washed over the table, wetting Ingvar's beautifully ironed trousers.

'Are you ashamed of your mother?' said Mum.

'Yes,' I said, and the nastiness inside me felt good.

Before I disappeared out through the front door I glanced in the big hall mirror. In it I saw a thin, tall and insignificant short-haired girl, wearing a pair of patched jeans, gym shoes and a stripy jumper, with badness shining from her eyes. I grabbed my pink jacket and left.

If Mum looked like some sort of queen of the jungle, I looked more like a half-famished suburban rat.

Obviously I was late for my first day at my new school. It took time to find that pile of bricks by the water with a fenced schoolyard and a statue that looked a lot like a barbecued chicken. Then I had to find the right classroom as well.

When I opened the door, the whole class stared at me as if I was something that was part of the lesson, like a stuffed bird or something. All the people I didn't know the names of sat there – there was Sieve and Fish, Sofia, Nettie, Para, Danny, Pepsi, Klara, Ant, Skunk and Isaac and Berra and Kati and the others – all of them looking at me.

The teacher was quite old and looked plump and nice. She was wearing a cream-coloured, flouncy summer dress and looked pretty much like a cream puff. She smiled with small strawberry-red lips.

'You must be the new person in our class?' she said.

'I suppose so,' I said, trying to sound cool.

'You should have come yesterday. Isn't that correct?'

What could I say to that? I couldn't tell her that yesterday my grandpa arrived from the rest home in a pair of ladies' boots to die in our house! That wouldn't go down well. So it was six of one and half a dozen of the other. If I told her the truth, no one would believe me. You have to lie to be believed.

'I got lost,' I said, lamely.

I heard straight away how stupid it sounded.

Bugger! The first thing I did was look like the world's biggest super-nerd. I heard people giggling and could sense them grinning and squirming in their seats. I hadn't started very well.

'If you've walked so far, then maybe you'd better sit down and rest,' said the teacher nicely. 'You can sit by the window.'

I had hoped for a place right up the back corner, where I would be able to take things easy and check out the others. But no. I had to sit almost up the front. Not only that, but next to the toughest and most superior of all – quite a big guy with blond, tousled hair, light blue eyes and a face sprinkled with lots of freckles which hadn't quite made it out for the season.

It was Isaac.

'My name's Isaac,' he said, smiling.

'What are you grinning at, you moron!' I hissed back.

After a while the classroom was quiet.

'Okay then,' said the teacher, whose name was Gudrun Baker. 'Let's welcome the new boy, Simon Kroll, to our class. I hope you will enjoy it here, both with me and with your classmates.'

The new boy! Simon!

Suddenly I realized she was talking about me. That strange name of mine, Simone, had got me into trouble again. I was so tired of it all I wanted to weep. I always had to repeat my name. Why had I not been called Frida or Anna or Christina or Linda instead?

'Simone is a very beautiful French name,' Mum usually said when I complained. It's possible. But I didn't want a beautiful French name. I wanted a normal, Swedish name that people didn't ask me to repeat again and again, staring at me hard as if you have to be something special to have a name like that. I wanted a name you could be grey and dull and ugly with.

Someone must have heard it wrong or written it wrong. Simone had lost its 'e' at the end. Here they were expecting a boy called Simon. And then I turned up! What should I do now? For someone so normal, I was having a lot of bad luck when it came to ending up in impossible situations.

Should I tell the truth? 'Excuse me, but there must be a mistake? I'm a girl, actually. My name is not Simon, it's Simone.' It was impossible. I knew what would happen. They would all fall off their seats laughing. I would be cast out for ever. And I would still get called Simon or 'little fancy pants' or something equally hilarious.

I carefully felt my short curls and tried to remember what I'd looked like in the mirror. My hair was short enough and I had no clips or ribbons or anything that would give me away. It was lucky I hadn't started to get breasts like some of the others. Or that I hadn't pulled on a dress this morning. My clothes could just as easily be worn by a boy. Apart from my undies of course, but they weren't to be seen, luckily.

'Thanks,' I said as hoarsely and boyishly as I could. 'I'm sure I'll like it here.'

The cream cake up the front smiled beatifically with her strawberry lips.

'Greaser,' hissed the boy next to me who was called Isaac.

'Rat piss,' I whispered.

'Hairy arse,' he said, and against my will I felt momentarily impressed by his inventiveness.

'Skunk bum!' I said.

'Toad face,' he countered with lightning speed.

Then the teacher put a stop to it. And it was just as well. I reckon he would've beaten me hands down if we'd carried on. I felt I would come to hate this boy.

'I understand you're anxious to get to know each other,' she glowed. She had seen our lips moving and thought we were whispering small pleasantries to each other. 'But you can continue to talk at break.'

'By the way, Isaac,' she added, 'it would be very nice if you would like to show Simon around a little here at school, as you are already getting on so well together.'

Isaac nodded enthusiastically at the teacher and tried to look like a good Big Brother, at the same time his hand searched under the desk and gave my thigh a horse-bite which stung like a thousand wasp stings.

Even though it hurt I felt a rush of joy. I had tricked all of them. They had fallen for it! No one seemed to doubt for a second that I was really who they thought I was.

I had quickly and easily been freed from being that girl Simone who always got into trouble, and instead become a nasty troublemaker by the name of Simon.

If only I'd known what that would bring with it.

When the bell rang I grabbed a bleached jean jacket from a hook at the end of the corridor.

It was several sizes too big and covered in studs. 'Motörhead' was written in big silver letters on the back. It sagged over my thin body and smelled of dirt and petrol and tobacco. It was a find. I would have to get rid of the pink jacket I'd worn on the way here as quickly as possible.

'Don't think I'm going to be some sort of Daddy to you,' said Isaac.

He came up to me as I stood leaning against the barbecued chicken made of steel, which actually turned out to be not a broiler but a dead horse with its legs in the air. The whole yard was full of ducks waddling around waiting for us to throw them bits of school food. It was forbidden. But everybody did it.

'I don't need any sort of Daddy,' I said, spitting at one of the ducks.

'That's good. Just as long as you don't get any ideas.'

'I don't have any ideas. But shouldn't you get started?'

'Get started with what?'

'You're a bit slow, aren't you?'

'What do you mean by that?'

'You have to keep asking the same question the whole time.'

'You're impossible to talk to!'

I can carry on like that forever. I'm good at it. Isaac looked cross and I was pleased. I smiled the crooked sort of smile I had seen boys do. Isaac turned around to leave.

'Is he always like that?' I wondered out loud.

'Like what?' said a girl with thick glasses. She blew her gum into a little pink balloon which burst in her face.

'Unfriendly,' I said. 'He's supposed to show me around.'

'Yes, you are supposed to do that, Isaac. The teacher said so,' said the girl, trying to get rid of the sticky threads with her nails.

Isaac didn't answer. He just looked at her in a way that meant he was sorry she sounded as boring as she looked. He started to leave. I followed. I went close, close behind him and tramped on his heels.

'What are you doing?' he hissed.

'I'm following you in case you haven't noticed, numbskull,' I said and carried on tramping on his heels so that he tripped forwards.

'Well stop it, you idiot!' he yelled.

'Won't,' I said. 'You're supposed to show me round. So now you'd better do it.'

The sun shone on my neck and the ducks quacked happily over leftovers of hard bread, fish balls and blood pudding. A light breeze came from the lake. A whole group of rubber-neckers had gathered around us. I saw the bubblegum girl with glasses standing beside a girl with a short-short skirt and long legs, a little mouth and big breasts, small nose and big eyes. Half the class was there.

I carried on walking on Isaac's heels and I knew that soon he wouldn't tolerate any more. I could feel the expectation in the eyes following us and I felt a bubbling expectation myself.

Suddenly he spun round, wild eyed, and tried to hit me in the mouth as if he was hammering a nail into a plank. It was a heavy, clumsy hit that wasn't hard to dodge. I grabbed his arm and went down in a spin, so that he rolled over my back and hit the asphalt nose-first. It was a move Grandpa had taught me, one of those summers now so long ago.

Isaac got to his feet and for a moment we stood facing each other. We were almost the same height. Except he was broader than me. We looked in each other's eyes. I saw that he thought this was as much fun as I did.

Suddenly he fell on me and pushed me to the ground. I got his elbow on my lip so it burst. I tasted blood and smelt lilac. And when I looked up I saw that the girl with the breasts was smiling at me and looking at me in a very special way.

It was Kati.

Beside her was the Dove, the phys ed teacher – except I didn't know that then. But I wasn't stupid enough not to know that he was a teacher.

'What are you up to, boys?' he said coldly.

'He slipped on some duck poo and hit his nose,' I said, pointing to Isaac. 'And when I went to help him I fell as well and hurt my lip.'

'And what's your name?' asked the Dove.

'Simon,' I said.

'I'll remember that. Go on and clean yourselves up now.'

We went together to the boys' toilets. Neither of us said anything.

For a moment I was close to standing beside Isaac at the urinal, I was so swept up in my new role as a boy. Then I realized there were actually some things I couldn't do.

That afternoon, the sun shone in through the window. You could see a glimpse of sea behind the gym, as blue as the writing pad Mrs Baker, called the Bun, had given me. Swallows swooped across the sky and I sucked my bottom lip which tasted of salt and was slowly swelling to a fantastic size. Out of the corner of my eye I could see the stuck-up Isaac rubbing his scraped nose.

'Want to play noughts and crosses, mouse brain?' I wrote on a piece of paper I ripped from my writing pad and sent over to Isaac. He drew a cross on a grid and sent it back.

We played ten times while the Bun talked about pets and asked which of us had pets at home. I won eight times and Isaac looked really cross. I lost twice, mostly because I started thinking about Kilroy when the Bun asked me, and I said I had a dog. Where was he now? Would I see him again? Maybe I didn't have a dog anymore.

Almost everyone in the class seemed to have some sort of pet. Frida said she had a parrot. Kati said she had a Shetland pony even though it lived in the country. Ant had a budgie, Pepsi had an Alsatian. Nettie had a cat and Fish had fish in an aquarium. Stefan said he had a bat, though it was injured in one wing so his father had killed it. Dannie had rabbits in a hutch in the garden and Anna – the girl with the glasses and the chewing gum – had a walking stick.

'Birds,' said Isaac, when the Bun asked him.

When she asked him what sort he said he couldn't remember what they were called. But they were brown, he said. The Bun said it would be nice if some people could bring their pets to school. I hoped she wouldn't ask me. How could you bring a disappeared dog? But she asked Isaac instead.

'Sure,' he said.

When the final bell rang, Isaac stood waiting.

I had gone slowly on purpose. I didn't want to risk bumping into the owner of the jean jacket I'd stolen in the corridor. Judging by its size, it belonged to a big guy. So I stayed behind in class while the others burst out like dandelion seeds into the sunshine.

'Which way are you going?' he said, pretending to be friendly.

What did he want? Probably he wanted to trick me a bit and then smash me into a ditch. He was that sort.

'The other direction,' I said coldly.

'Which other?' he said.

'The one you're not going in,' I said.

He looked admiringly at my jacket. He clearly wasn't about to give up.

'Where'd you get that?' he asked.

Did he know something? Maybe he'd been sent by the guy who owned the jacket. Then out of the corner of my eye I saw a jacketless guy, his stomach wobbling under his T-shirt, coming in our direction. He looked about the same size as the jacket, and his face reminded me of those bulldogs that run up and eat the ears of innocent small dogs in the comics I read when I was little. His arms gleamed white and cold. They were big and gnarled, as if they lifted weights and swung ski poles in the evenings.

I looked at Isaac and I felt the ill wind blow inside me.

'Do you like it?' I asked.

He nodded.

'Here, take it. I'm tired of it anyway.'

I wriggled out of the jacket and threw it at him. He looked surprised and started to cram his arms into the unlucky garment. All the time the plump body-building figure was drawing nearer. He had clearly seen the jacket. He stopped and looked confused as a thought squeezed its way into his skull. Soon he would realize it was his jacket, and the realization would sink down through his thick neck, into his leg muscles and then he would get up to speed. I didn't plan on sticking around.

'Thanks … But …' stammered Isaac and didn't know what else to say.

'Bye! Gotta go!' I said, starting to run.

'Wait! Can't we be friends?' I heard him call behind me.

'No!' I called happily.

I jogged over the freshly-mown lawn down to the lake. Dandelions waved and buttercups shone, and thistles and nettles made stinging red patches over my shins and I breathed in the cool air from the water.

'How was school?' called Mum as soon as I stepped over the threshold.

'Normal,' I called back, hoping she wouldn't ask more.

I didn't feel like telling her that I had transformed into a boy; that her daughter had surprisingly become a son.

From my room upstairs I could hear Grandpa's cello sounding like the gentle snores of a lightly-dreaming god.

Ingvar was perched on a black stool in the living room. He was wearing a sort of wedding dress with a train that billowed over the cork tiles like a sparkling slalom slope. On his head was a white hat with a veil which partially concealed a pained expression – a mixture of constipation, dizziness and fear that Grandpa would come downstairs and catch him dressed unsuitably yet again. One arm was outstretched gracefully. In his hand was a white parasol.

'Can't you wear something a bit more feminine?' he said when he saw me.

Mum was in the middle of drawing him. Except she had the decency to leave out his face. She was an illustrator for all sorts of women's magazines – from popular ones to some more sordid. That was what we lived on. And because she didn't have any other models, Ingvar and I had to take turns.

'Maybe I could borrow a dress from you?' I smiled sweetly at him.

'Close your nasty little mouth, darling,' said Mum. 'I don't understand why you always have to tease Ingvar. Go and put on the potatoes instead. I am dy-yyying of hunger.'

'Sure,' I said.

On my way past Ingvar, the ill wind took hold of the train and spun him around like a desperate ice princess on his stool.

I had managed to peel my third potato before I heard the crash.

fifth chapter

I think things over, do some shopping, rediscover an old acquaintance and get blamed for something I didn't do

The train hacked and screeched away from Mum and Ingvar. A sad shimmer hung over the southern suburbs with their crazy apartments, small parks with slides and see-saws, rows of unwashed three-storey flats and small posh villas. The afternoon sun flashed in the windows and I thought about things.

How would this end? Things just kept on happening. And the more time went by, the more impossible everything became. My situation wasn't exactly brilliant.

How long could I convince people at school that I was a boy? What would happen if I got caught out? I shuddered at the thought. One, two, three and my breasts would suddenly sprout, and then what? Although maybe you could bind them. Like they did with little girls' feet in China.

Starting from now, I had to live a risky double life. At home I was still a little girl about to grow up. At school and in front of my new friends, I was a boy. Imagine if any of my classmates wanted to come home with me. And the same went for Mum wanting to shuttle off to school to speak to the teacher.

Phew!

The best thing would be for me to tell the truth first thing next day. 'Excuse me, I was just joking, actually I'm a girl ...' The more time passed, the more I would get myself tied up in knots.

No, I couldn't! I couldn't stand the thought of what would happen if I told the truth. That would make that stroppy, up-himself moron Isaac feel really smart. And what would that well-meaning creamcake of a teacher think? She'd think I was a right twaddle-face.

All in all: things would have to carry on as they were.

And, obviously, everything was the fault of the hat idiot!

He had started everything. If he hadn't decided to get together with Mum, we would never have moved into the draughty wooden house beside the rubbish dump. Then we would never have lost Kilroy. I would still be going to my old school and I wouldn't have to be a boy. Mum and I would go on small springtime expeditions with our basketful of fizzy drink and sausages, like we used to.

By the time I'd got this far in my thinking the train had reached Central Station and it was time for me to get off.

I took the elevator back up into the light and the wind and the terrible electric organ that piped Salvation Army songs into the square.

Ingvar had given me money to buy some new clothes. Since I'd lost the Motörhead jacket, I had to get something new in the same style.

'Get yourself something nice and sweet,' Ingvar had said as I left.

'Yeah-hh,' I managed, and smiled a glorious false smile.

I wandered around aimlessly, looking in the windows.

The afternoon sun was cold and I shivered in my T-shirt. I slunk into the small street behind the sports shop. It was lined with strange shops. Music blasted from them and the shelves were full of fantastic cowboy boots, Peter Pan shoes, glass beads, men's trousers, lingerie and military jackets.

At Impo, I found a scruffy jacket and a pair of black jeans. They would have to do. I pulled on my new clothes and walked back up to the square again.

Then I came upon a place called Ohio. It smelt of leather and hair cream, and the walls were plastered with posters of tough-looking hard-rock groups, and on the sign was a pair of entwined leather whips.

It was just the sort of boutique I needed.

I looked at all the sweatshirts, badges, hair bands and buttons. I chose a nice sweatshirt with 'Iron Maiden' on it in bleeding letters. Under the words was a purple devil dancing over a sea of purple flames. I also bought a black belt which looked like a dog collar. It was covered in pointy studs. I completed my purchases with a similar bracelet and some Kiss and Scorpion badges. I put all this on and felt very pleased with myself.

No one would ever mistake me for an innocent little girl!

I had just finished paying for the final item – a pair of Olympia Y-fronts – when I saw something that made my heart stop. I froze.

Over by the Orpheus fountain was a scruffy, grey-white dog with drooping ears and a sad tail, peeing against the side of the pool.

It was Kilroy!

But you should have seen what he looked like! Hungry and skinny and sick. He put his leg back down and loped away to the fruit and vegetable stand. He was probably looking for something to eat among all the rubbish on the ground.

'Kilroy! Kilroy! For pete's sake, Kilroy!' I yelled like a mad woman.

People turned and stared at me, as I hurtled between women with bags full of shopping, children, businessmen with black briefcases, and a gang of yowling weirdos with shaved heads, small bells and orange rags wrapped round their bodies. The clattering, whining song of the shaved-head people drowned out my shouts.

Just when I had really got up speed and was thinking I might catch Kilroy, a straggly, grey-haired loser appeared from one of the paths between the buildings, flying on a pair of roller skates.

He was holding a big sign with STOP CRUEL TESTING ON ANIMALS written on it.

I didn't have a chance of getting out of his way.

His left skate caught my right boot. Like an injured moose, I stumbled through a crowd of shoulders and breasts and stomachs until at last I lost my balance completely. I searched for something to break my fall. By instinct, I grabbed at the thing in front of me.

'Help! My bag! Help! I've been robbed! Someone come and help!' I heard someone screaming above me.

The voice belonged to an old woman with a black coat and a brown felted pillbox hat. She stood there with her legs shaking, pointing at me on the ground still clutching her brown suede bag.

Now things were looking really good!

'I've been robbed! Won't anyone help me?' the woman kept calling.

I struggled to my feet and hung the bag back on the accusing arm. It hung there, dangling like a little flag.

'I'm sorry, it was a mistake,' I said wearily. 'I fell and just happened to grab hold of your bag to keep my balance. I didn't mean to.'

A group of curious people had gathered.

'What's going on here?' I heard someone say.

'That boy just tried to steal this lady's handbag,' another answered. 'He's drunk as well. He can't stand up straight.'

'Isn't it terrible? He's just a child. How can anyone attack an old woman like that?'

The atmosphere was growing more threatening by the moment.

'Young people are getting worse and worse,' said a voice I thought I recognized.

Looking over, I saw Mr Axelsson. He had pushed to the front of the line and was watching the drama intently. Axelsson was our closest neighbour. He lived in a house clad in hideous grey tiles, right next door to ours, alone with his cat and some bees.

Had he recognized me? Absolutely, I could see in his eyes that he had.

'I've seen that one before,' he said, pleased to have something to say. 'He lives out by me. Just moved in.

Very nice neighbours, I must say.'

'Don't you understand it was a mistake?' I pleaded. 'I didn't mean to take the bag. I fell over a roller skater and grabbed hold of it on my way down.'

I tried to wriggle away through the small crowd of onlookers. But a solid man in a homemade jumper grabbed me by the shoulder. 'You can stay right here, young man,' he said. 'You're not going anywhere.'

Looking through a gap in the crowd, I glimpsed Kilroy wandering over the street, with his head hanging down and his tail between his legs. I couldn't let him disappear again!

But he did.

I tried to break free from the grip on my shoulder, but couldn't get anywhere. Now the police had turned up! A policewoman stood with a pear in her hand.

'What's going on here?' she said.

'About time,' sighed Axelsson. 'Here he is! This boy tried to steal a handbag from the little old lady, the animal. And he's drunk. You can arrest him.'

But the policewoman wasn't in a hurry. First of all she patted the shocked old lady and worked out that she had her handbag back and that nothing was missing. Then she asked everyone what had happened. She found the roller skate man on the steps of the Concert Hall trying to gather up all his damaged leaflets. He said it was true that I had come rushing right in front of him. What had happened afterwards he knew nothing about. He had crashed into a display of women's underwear.

I told her everything – how I had caught a glimpse of Kilroy, how I had sprinted and fallen over the roller skate man and grabbed hold of a handbag without knowing what it was.

The policewoman took a bite of her pear every now and then. There was a hard-to-decipher smile playing at the edges of her mouth. I had the feeling she was finding it hard not to laugh.

In many people's eyes I was already doomed. The worst of all was Axelsson.

'Nothing here to argue about, eh?' he said. 'All you have to do is to put that delinquent kid away, eh? What he needs is a good long time in prison, eh? And what was all that rubbish he told her? Women shouldn't be police. They should stay at home and make sure their children don't thieve handbags, eh?'

Suddenly the policewoman grabbed me under the arm and pushed decisively through the crowd.

'Best you come with me!' she said in a harsh voice, pulling me with her. 'No tricky business now!'

It was all over! If everything hadn't felt so unreal, I would have started to cry. Who would believe me? I followed her passively along the street. Behind me, the crowd started to disperse. What would happen to me now? She would probably carry on asking me questions at the police station. They would ring home, of course. How would Mum take it? Would she believe me? Everything felt shaky. Ingvar would say I was guilty, naturally. The worst thing would be if Mum thought that I would really rob an innocent old lady. Then I would have nobody.

I was so far away in my thoughts that I jumped when

I felt a hand stroking my cheek.

'How are you doing? What have you got such a long face for then?' I heard a soft voice at my side. 'Good to be rid of those people, don't you think?'

I must have looked ridiculous, because the policewoman burst into ringing laughter.

'Did you think I was going to put you in prison, you little ninny? I'm sorry if I was a bit heavy-handed. But I thought it was the best way to get us out of the lion's den,' she said.

She held me lightly by the arm and walked with a springing step.

'That was a truly crazy story,' she continued. 'With a bit of bad luck, you could have ended up at the police station. But now I wonder if we couldn't have a look for your dog instead.'

We combed the town without finding a trace of Kilroy. He had disappeared. But at least he was still alive. If it was him. But in the end, when we had covered the whole neighbourhood, we had to give up.

Before I disappeared into the underground to go home, the policewoman waved at me.

'Take care of yourself!' she called.

When I came home it had already started to get dark. Ingvar was out at a meeting. It was nice. Mum had taken her saxophone up to Grandpa. I could hear them playing together upstairs. Except it sounded more as if they were talking. The cello with its mild, dark voice and the saxophone, wild and soft at the same time, croaked and laughed and cried. They had a quiet conversation about things that words couldn't express. Together they had played their way back to a time and a friendship long before I was born.

I stuck my newly purchased badges to my jacket with fabric glue and pressed them on firmly with the iron. Then I made myself a cup of tea with honey and milk and snuggled down into the mahogany monster. I pulled the covers over my face and tried to have peace and quiet. But it was hopeless. My thoughts were going around in circles, like bats in my head.

It was four days since my twelfth birthday and already I felt years older. It was as if I'd been thrown onto a carousel which kept going faster and faster. What would happen now?

I took the crystal ball which had once belonged to Grandpa's mother. The rosy, shimmering evening light shone into the ball and made it glow. A swaying tree outside the window made the ball look like a little lighthouse going on and off, on and off. After a while it came to life like a crazy small projector, and showed a whole lot of random images: a flock of white flapping birds; dark storm clouds; a leg in plaster; Grandpa's summer house on the island; a swan; rushing water … Then it turned off again and lay cold and dark on the bedspread. I tapped it. But it wouldn't come back to life.

I pushed the ball to the foot of the bed, turned to the wall and tried to sleep with my eyes open.

sixth chapter

I get ready, Isaac gets revenge, we visit the boatshed and I almost forget who I am

'Aren't you ready yet? What are you doing in there?' Ingvar cried in desperation.

He banged on the toilet door so that all Mum's jars and bottles in the bathroom cupboard hopped up and down.

If there was anything that made Ingvar mad, it was not being able to get into the toilet when his bowels said it was time.

I flushed the toilet to settle him down and cut off more curls with the kitchen scissors. They fell into the hand basin which was now full of dark brown hair.

'Calm down! I'll be finished soon!' I yelled at the door.

I looked at myself in the mirror and was pleased with what I saw. I had made my hair shorter by another few centimetres. Now my head looked like one of those Monchhichi monkeys. Even though it was a little bit uneven in some places, it was quite funky. It made my face look longer and my eyes bigger.

'Are you living in there?' shouted Ingvar.

'He who waits for something good never waits too long,' I said rudely and swept up the hair and flushed it away with a pathetic flush which meant that the cistern was still filling.

I was wearing my new clothes and was ready to greet the new day as a boy. Just when I was about to unlock the door and let Ingvar in, I thought of something. I grabbed a handful of cotton balls from the bag by the hand-towel and rolled them into a sausage-shaped ball which I shoved inside the fly on my Y-fronts. It was important not to miss any details.

'At last!' Ingvar cried and he burst over the threshold when I opened the door.

Then he stopped in his tracks with a shocked look on his face.

'Good God, look at you, girl!' he said. 'What have you done to your hair? And what are you wearing?'

'You said I should buy something sweet and nice,' I said innocently.

'Are you planning to go to school like that? What will the teacher say?'

'All the girls in the class look like this,' I lied. 'The teacher does, too.'

Then I disappeared. I didn't want to get into any long discussions. I swung past the kitchen and grabbed a couple of bananas and a mandarin before shooting out into the cold, grey, May weather.

The Bun was up the front of the class. She was wearing her long-distance glasses so she could make sure that no one cheated. Her eyes swam around like a pair of wakeful piranhas behind her glasses. We had been made to move our desks apart. A quiet scraping of pencils and rubbers could be heard. Otherwise it was quiet.

I cast a look at Isaac. He was leaning over his paper with his pen drilled up one nostril and looked like he was having trouble with the questions.

Good! It served him right. He hadn't even looked at me since he came rushing into school in a red jeep just as the school bell rang for the second time. His father looked as stuck-up as he was, sitting at the wheel and tooting so that everyone could see how wonderful they looked, the jeep and Isaac and him.

Isaac had one ear that was red and swollen, and a new swollen lip, better than mine. That muscle-bound guy, worried about his jean jacket, had clearly given him a real work-over yesterday. My evil-filled heart was joyous. Now he had something to keep him quiet.

I was already finished. English was my favourite subject. No one had told me that we were going to have a test today, but I managed with what I already knew, from my previous life as a quiet and clever girl. I had time to look around me.

One wall was covered in a whole lot of drawings. Most of them were tacky: Donald Duck; guitar players; trees; and houses with billowing chimneys and flags sticking straight out. Fish had drawn a moped, Dannie a green snake and Kati a girl with huge breasts.

One drawing stood out from all the others.

It was a white swan flying in over blue-grey water with its feet surfing, so that it made a scum of white bubbles in the grey. The wings were outstretched, filled with air, and the throat bent forwards. I don't know what it was that made the picture so fantastic. Maybe because it was so precise; it so exactly captured a moment which would have disappeared in a second. The white swan looked like an angel in the midst of all the grey, floating between a grey sky and the grey sea.

When I looked carefully I saw that the name 'Isaac' was written in the right-hand corner.

At the same moment, someone tapped me on the shoulder. It was Isaac. When I turned around he threw a screwed up piece of paper at my desk. Had he lost his mind? Did he think the Bun was completely blind? I never thought he would be that clumsy! He might be good at drawing, but he was useless at cheating.

The Bun's eyes glimmered behind her glasses.

With surprising speed considering the shape of her body, she came over to Isaac while her right hand swung down like a meat axe and snatched the piece of paper.

She was panting with rage and not the slightest bit like a creamcake.

'Are you sitting there and cheating right in front of my nose?' she hissed and grabbed hold of Isaac. 'What is the meaning of this?'

I almost felt sorry for Isaac. It couldn't be fun to meet the force of the Bun's rage.

'I haven't cheated,' he said clearly.

That was probably the worst thing he could have said. It was obvious that he was trying to get out of it. It wasn't often someone got caught so blatantly. It would have been better to admit to it and try to look sorry.

'What?' she said and panted even harder. 'Are you going to lie as well? There are two things I will not accept under any circumstances. One is cheating. And the other is lying. You, Isaac, have just been caught out on both counts. You should be ashamed!'

'I'm not ashamed because I haven't cheated,' he said stubbornly.

He must be a bit stupid. Or else he wanted to make her mad on purpose. But what did he have to gain from that?

The room was completely silent. Everyone had put down their pens. Everyone except Anna, who chewed the end of her pen then carried on writing. With painful slowness, the Bun lifted the note into the air. She waved it a little, making a face as if she held a snotty handkerchief.

'And what is this?' she asked. 'A little love note, perhaps?'

'Not really,' said Isaac.

'Then we will see what is written on the note,' she said. 'Maybe you would like to read it yourself, Isaac?'

'The teacher can read it,' said Isaac.

She smoothed out the crumpled piece of paper and glanced through its contents. What a bugger that I hadn't had time to grab it and chew it up while it was still on my desk! The Bun stopped still with the note in her hand and we all waited to see what would happen next.

'I am sorry,' she said in a toneless voice. 'You must forgive me, Isaac. I was too quick to judge. Now we will all hear what is on the note. This is what it says: "No way, Simon, I don't want to cheat, you gutter rat! Try someone else. Signed, Isaac."'

I felt my stomach sink. My God he was smart! By seeming so clumsy with that note, he got me to look like the world's worst cheat! I was stuck tight on the hook. There was nothing to gain by trying to explain it. It was watertight. I shivered and felt my respect for this cunning fiend grow.

The Bun turned to me.

'It was you I should have told off instead,' she said.

She grabbed my test that I had shifted to one side and tore it into tiny, little pieces which floated down to the floor.

'That's what we'll do with your paper, Simon,' she said. 'We can talk about it further at break.'

I looked at Isaac and met his gaze. He smiled a crazy smile full of joy and warm-heartedness. He had got his revenge. Now we were even!

'What did she say?'

We sat down by the lake, at a safe distance from school. The wind off the water was cold and we had taken cover in a dilapidated boatshed. It had been used once upon a time for storing oars and other boat accessories, when you could hire boats for small Sunday excursions. A pair of rotten oars was still here from that time.

Otherwise Isaac, Dannie, Fish, Stefan and Pepsi had decorated the old shed with things they had brought here from the rubbish tip – a wobbly tent bed, a little table, a battery radio which the technical whiz-kid Pepsi had fixed so it crackled out music and weather reports, the time and agricultural programmes in a constant stream. There were also a few wooden chairs, a kerosene lamp, an old iron stove and a primus.

On the table was a pile of old comics, an almost full pack of cards, and some pornographic magazines. The floor was covered with cigarette butts and trampled chewing gum.

It was on the whole a very nice locale where no girls were allowed. Except for Kati, of course. Because she let the boys squeeze her breasts and told them dirty stories about what grown-ups did with each other at night.

Fish had brought a bunch of roll-your-own tobacco with him.

We sucked in the harsh, prickly smoke. It made your stomach go round like a cement mixer so that the mixture of potatoes, white sauce and pork pieces tossed around inside. We all tried to look as if we felt great and couldn't think of anything better to do than to puff on those stinking vomit sticks.

It was as if all their suspicion about me had blown away. They had gathered around me at break, full of sympathy and curiosity, and with the kind of admiration you can expect when you've made an adult lose her cool.

I was suddenly someone to count on.

Isaac himself had taken me to the shed. It was so secret that there always had to be a guard on duty at the door, to make sure that no idiots, telltales, girls or teachers would find it.

Now I was one of the guys in the gang. The bad wind that had blown its way into me giggled happily.

While Dannie scraped away the remains of a lovely scab on his knee with a pocket knife, I told one of the world's biggest cock-and-bull stories about how angry the Bun had been. Everyone grinned happily, and knew that it was lies. In actual fact, she had wondered if I had any problems and looked at me with big, worried eyes. But there was no need to tell anyone that. I would have almost preferred it if she had been angry. Those eyes made me nervous.

Isaac giggled too. He didn't say anything about how the whole thing had been his doing. That he had led me to the gallows. And I had no reason to say anything either. If he wanted to show off about how clever he was, that was his thing. On the other hand, I could tell them about the Motörhead jacket. He had something on me and I had something on him.

I squinted at him while he sat and spat out some bits of tobacco that had got stuck in his mouth. And I started to wonder if maybe I had been wrong. Maybe he wasn't the stuck-up total moron that I thought he was.

'What shall I do?' he said when I had finished. 'The Bun has been on to me about bringing my birds with me tomorrow.'

'What should you do … Can't you take them with you?' Fish suggested, trying to look clever.

'That's what I would do. If I had any,' said Isaac.

'You don't have any?' said Fish. 'Why did you say you did then?'

'No idea,' said Isaac. 'It just happened.'

I understood him completely. I had said that I had a dog. Even though Kilroy had disappeared.

'Say they've flown away,' I suggested.

'I should have said that straight away,' said Isaac gloomily. 'But I was so surprised when she asked me that I promised to bring them.'

'Nah, tomorrow say that they look sick,' said Stefan.

'She won't believe me,' said Isaac.

'I'll sort it,' I said, before I had really thought about it. 'I'll make sure you have your birds in the classroom tomorrow morning.'

'How's that?' Isaac's eyebrows were raised.

'My secret,' I said, wondering how in the world I would manage it.

At the same time there was a terrible clanging noise.

The old alarm clock on the table had set off a din, warning us to make it back to school in time.

It was finally time to stub out those horrible cigarettes.

I didn't hurry back. I had to pee. And I wanted to do it in peace.

I felt very pleased with myself. The only thing I regretted was promising to take those birds.

When I came to the gymnasium, the others had already started to get changed. The Dove looked cross. He hopped up and down a bit to warm himself.

'Go in and get changed,' he cried. 'Don't be slow about it, since you are already late!'

Where would I get the birds from? Did I know anyone I could borrow some from? I definitely didn't know anyone with brown birds. Was it brown birds he said he had?

I was so absorbed in my thoughts that I didn't notice anything strange. Suddenly I heard screaming and shouting around me. A whole lot of half-naked girls were hopping around. They were waving their underwear and trousers and singlets and trying to hide behind them. Anna hit me right on the bum with one of those rubber boots her mother sent her off with in case it rained.

Kati was the only one who kept calm. She came giggling towards me and jiggled a little so that her breasts wobbled up and down.

Why were they carrying on like this? Who were they hiding from? Then I realised. I had wandered into the girls' changing room. I had forgotten I was a boy. What a dork! Lucky I hadn't whipped my clothes off as well.

'Out! Get out of here, you peeping tom!' cried Frida, pulling a pair of underpants over my head. I couldn't see anything.

Then someone took my arm. Anna was going to swing at me with one of those foot-shaped rubber batons. I kicked the shins of whoever had got hold of me.

'Let go, for pete's sake! Or you'll be sorry!' I said, as tough as I could.

There was a surprised grunt when my shoe connected. It wasn't very girlish.

'Are you out of your mind, you little monster?' roared a deep voice.

It was the Dove! He dragged me through the door. I slumped after him like a sack of sand. The knickers travelled up my forehead. I could feel them sitting like a little lace cap on top.

The Dove looked at me with his eyes full of distaste. I didn't look the way one of 'his boys' should.

'I will lick you into shape. Trust me, Simon!' he said with a sinister tone.

I had to sit in the boys' changing room for the rest of the hour. What a punishment! If only the Dove had known.

I sat on a bench with my arms around me, breathing in the exhilarating smells of sweat and old gym shoes. After a while the Dove's whistle blasted through the grunting, yelling and squeaking of gym shoes. The boys raced in. They pulled off their sweaty phys ed gear and sprang naked into the showers. I glanced happily at their willies that hopped between their legs like cocktail sausages, radishes and small carrots.

Without anyone seeing, I snuck my hand down to touch the ball of cotton in my pants. It sat where it should!

seventh chapter

Someone keeps me company, an unwanted kiss has unbelievable consequences, Mum is cross and Grandpa talks about night demons

Suddenly she was just there.

Without me knowing, she'd glided to my side. She was like a cat. Her body was smooth and silent, padding along on soft Nike-paws. Her gold eyes sparkled and her mouth was shaped to a little bow.

'Can I walk with you a bit?' she asked.

It was Kati.

I nodded without saying anything. It wouldn't have made any difference if I had. She would have done what she wanted to anyway.

I had thought that my trial was over. Happily and obliviously, I had been whistling one of those melodies that Grandpa often stroked out of his old cello. I had made some preparations for the bird-catching. I had unhooked the window to our classroom before I left. So it wouldn't blow open, I had put a wad of paper in the gap.

In our part of town, everything was named after birds – the streets were named Gull and Buzzard and Owl and so on. I had got as far as Cuckoo Street when Kati appeared like a pink shadow with some sort of plastic, pale blue handbag slung over her shoulder, and her earphones like a stethoscope around her neck. She took hold of my arm and blew small puffs of Juicy Fruit over my face.

'I'm going that way too,' she said, pointing vaguely in a few directions.

'Mmm,' I said.

She smiled with her pointy little teeth and I started to feel nervous.

I had the feeling that it was more dangerous to be with girls than it was with boys. I didn't know how to act with them. I felt her breast against my elbow and I tried to think of a way to get rid of her. But I couldn't think of anything.

Do girls have more second sight than boys? Can they kind of sniff their way to things that guys have no idea about? Do they have a different sense of smell for things that almost go unnoticed? I thought about this while I was silent. And I decided it was true. And that calmed me down a bit. Kati would surely notice that something was odd about me, that I was just a badly-made forgery of a boy.

'You're not like the other guys,' she said and looked at me straight in the eyes.

Quite right. She had worked it out!

'Nah-hhh,' I said for something to say.

'You're kind of different somehow.'

'Mmm.'

'I don't know what it is.'

'Nah-hhh.' I was feeling more and more stupid.

'You're sort of, I don't know, more mature, somehow,' she said. 'The others are so childish. All except for Isaac, maybe. But it's hard to work him out really.

You seem more real than the others somehow. Am I making sense?'

'Mmm,' I said, but I was finding it hard not to laugh.

Me, more real! Me, the most terrible fake you could imagine. I pressed closer to Kati so she couldn't see how flummoxed I was. Our cheeks touched. She must have misunderstood the whole thing because she put her arm around my shoulders and her hair flicked over my face and tickled my top lip so that I had to smile. Then she turned towards me and smiled even more. And while I was busy thinking that maybe boys are playing boys and girls are playing girls in one big performance that never ends, I felt her hand stroke the Kiss badge on my shoulder.

The whole thing was completely idiotic. I had to maintain my facade. I just had to hang on a little bit longer. Soon I would be home. We had got as far as the Godwits. There were just the Finches, the Blackbirds and the Gulls to go!

We walked in silence for a while. I tried to take long, manly steps to win some time. Small birds chirped in the bushes and, from behind the rubbish tip, the gulls shrieked their long, drawn-out cries. Kati stuck to me like a shadow right up the last hill.

'I like you,' she said, when we stopped outside our gate.

Cripes! That was just what I needed.

'Mmm,' I said stupidly.

From Axelsson's you could hear the motor mower.

'I saw right from the start that there was something special about you,' she said. 'From the moment you stepped into the classroom that day and you were late and said that you had gone the wrong way. Things seem to happen around you. Do you get it?'

Sure I got it. Since we had moved, the most extraordinary things had been happening around me. What I wanted most of all was for the craziness to just stop for a minute, so I could enjoy a completely normal, greyish, boring sort of afternoon with some fantastically boring homework and a nerdy English TV program, ideally a repeat. But it wasn't looking likely.

I nodded and started to undo the gate with my foot.

'Yeah, well this is where I live,' I said. 'Fun to have your company. But now I have to rush in. Bye!'

'Wait,' she said.

She had put down her bag, like a pale blue road-cone, in front of the gate. She grabbed hold of my arm, so I couldn't go anywhere.

'You have to listen to this song first,' she said. 'You can manage that.'

I nodded again. It seemed quite harmless.

She unravelled the cord and then put the headphones over my reddening ears. We stood facing each other joined by the cord which was so short that our noses almost touched. Suddenly the music started. Ulf Lundell's rasping voice, strengthened by a choir and batteries, banged straight into my skull.

In love and crazy, he sang. *In love and crazy again, in love and crazy, enough to stand for what you do. In love and crazy, in love and crazy again. That's all I want, day after day, till I am singing in the angels' choir …*

With the music pumping like hot water into my ears, making me feel wobbly, Kati threw her arms around my neck. I opened my mouth to tell her to stop, that the whole thing was a terrible mistake. But by then she had already shoved her face, her lips, against mine. And her pointy tongue glided like a raspberry ice block into my open mouth. My right hand, which I'd raised to protect myself, was resting against her pink breast.

Her eyes looked cheerfully and greedily into mine while Ulf Lundell sang like he was possessed, and I felt completely crazy with her mouth stuck to mine while her hand stroked my stubby curls. It was the first time someone had kissed me like that. And it was a girl!

I couldn't look into those gold eyes any longer. When I looked away I saw a little yellow car coming along at such a snail's pace that it had to be Ingvar. And there was I, in the arms of another girl! I saw his eyes beneath the nerdy hat. They grew wide when he saw it was me. When he puttered past, he turned his head and looked at us through the side window with his nose pressed against the glass so that he looked like a dressed-up pig.

Then the car spurted forwards and roared through Axelsson's hedge. He must have put his foot on the accelerator instead of the brake. The car had drilled a hole in the hedge. Through the hole I could see Axelsson's surprised face above his motor mower and the yellow car still sliding through the garden. Finally it ran over a couple of beehives, knocking off the roofs. A cloud of upset bees poured out.

In my ears, Ulf Lundell was singing that he liked to live in the open countryside where the winds blow fresh, and the larks fly high in the sky singing a wondrous tune. That was the last I heard.

In terror I bit Kati's tongue at the same moment the car hit the beehives. She made a small whimpering sound and let go of me. She pointed over at the car.

'Oh my God, what an idiot!'

'It's my mother's boyfriend!' I yelled, yanking the headphones off. In the open countryside created by Ingvar's car, I could see Axelsson making for the buckled radiator with his motor mower at full speed ahead, surrounded by a cloud of bees. He seemed determined to mow through the car, using his mower like a can opener. I didn't want to see any more. Ingvar had just got the car into reverse and was on his way towards Axelsson's main gate.

'Sorry! See you!' I called to Kati.

I felt her golden eyes on my neck as I leapt over the gate using the pale blue plastic handbag as my starting block. I could taste the salt of her blood in my mouth.

When I pulled the door open I realised why Kati was somehow so familiar. She was like Mum – with the same golden wild animal eyes, the same tough, fresh courage to do what she wanted without asking first.

Mum was in a miserable humour. I saw that straight away.

She was curled up on all fours by the Persian rug in the sitting room, with a scarf tied around her head like a pirate. Things were all around her: a coffee cup with sticky remains of what might be an egg toddy, a piece of bread and a plate of yoghurt and crystallised ginger, a bag of wine gums, colouring pencils, watercolour paints, screwed-up paper and a few other drawing things. A paintbrush in her right hand was dripping dark brown stains onto the floor. In her left was one of her black cigarettes. Her bum was raised like a plum-coloured volcano covered in a cloud of smoke.

Grandpa was rocking back and forth in the rocking chair. He strummed the end of his impressive nose with his index finger. The lions on the back of the chair smiled.

'Tee-hee,' Grandpa giggled. 'And what would you know about the joy of life, if I may ask?'

'Quiet now, you stupid old man, so I can get a bit of work done,' Mum muttered from the mat.

'What are you doing?' I asked.

Except that I knew. They were arguing.

I could remember their arguments from when I was little. I was brought up with them. They could challenge and grumble at each other for hours. They loved it.

'Your mother has to make a picture about the joy of life for a magazine. And now she is angry and cross because she doesn't know what that looks like, my dove,' Grandpa said. 'An angrier painter of the joy of life would be hard to find.'

'I am not cross!' grumbled Mum. 'It's just that your grandfather has taken pleasure in disturbing me all day. He's been sitting there rocking like a duck right beside me. It's making me seasick. How anyone can get anything done in this house is a mystery to me. See what it looks like!'

She swept her arm around the room at all the muddle she had managed to make.

At that moment, Ingvar arrived. He was greeted by a shower of colour from Mum's paintbrush when she swished around with her arm.

'Hi,' he said.

He seemed relatively unscathed. His suit was wrinkled, the little bit of hair he had left was sticking up as if he had just woken, and on the top of his head you could see a little red swelling, presumably from an angry bee.

He smiled at us lovingly.

He was carrying a small package, wrapped up in the ketchup-coloured car rug. From a fold, a little paw peeped out.

Ingvar looked quite nice and foolishly attractive in a way I had never seen before.

He must have got brain damage, I thought. He must have bumped his head on the front window and gone absolutely nuts! It was obvious. If he hadn't hit his head, he would have been furious. But now his face had got stuck in a terrible, inane smile as he stood and hugged the rolled-up rug to his chest.

Suddenly I remembered that I thought I saw Axelsson's cat disappear under the back wheel when Ingvar started to reverse towards the gate. Seeing that single paw, a terrible thought struck me. Axelsson's cat must have been run over, and he had wrapped it up in the rug.

'Guess what I've got here?' said Ingvar, with a strange, soft tone to his voice.

He took a couple of unsteady steps in my direction.

'Don't bring it here! I don't want to see it!' I screamed.

I felt really terrified. Who wouldn't, if a brain-damaged idiot wanted to show them a cat he had run over?

Then a wrinkly little nose stuck out of the rug.

A pair of big brown eyes looked around helplessly and ears drooped and swung as if they had been only half sewn on. Then a chubby mouth opened in a yawn that made the head disappear. It was a little puppy!

'I sort of thought that …' said Ingvar, taking another step in my direction.

But then the puppy managed to escape from its furry wrapping. It slid over the floor. It stopped for a moment, shaking itself so that the loose folds of skin moved in waves over its skinny body. Its stump of a tail pointed straight up. It wagged crookedly a couple of times. And then the puppy disappeared like a rolling, bouncing ball under the glass cabinet. It lay as far away as it could, with its bottom pressed to the wall. You could see its big eyes gleaming, like black shiny stones. It sneezed and snuffled from all the dust.

'I thought it could be for you, Simone,' said Ingvar, poking his hand under the cupboard. 'It's a little boxer. I bought it from a man at work. I know how sad you are about Kilroy … But it's probably time we gave up hope for him. When I heard that my workmate's boxer had puppies and, well, now that Kilroy's disappeared … I thought a little cuddly thing like this might make you happier. Oh, hell!'

He pulled his hand out and shook it.

The puppy had nipped his finger with its tiny knife-sharp teeth.

Was that why he had looked so foolish? Because he had a secret wrapped up in a car blanket? He had gone and bought me a puppy. It hurt when he mentioned Kilroy. What did he mean, give up hope? Did he mean that Kilroy was dead? I looked at the empty dog basket with the chewed-up piece of material in the bottom. I could still sense that Kilroy-smell of sun and salt and fish. And I knew I didn't want another dog instead!

I remembered how it was when I first got him.

Grandpa had brought him home inside his winter coat with fur on the inside. Kilroy had stuck out his pointy white nose from the dark coat. I was about six years old and was sick with the measles. Outside it was snowing and freezing.

'Here's some company for your measles,' Grandpa said, laughing. Since then Kilroy and I had been inseparable. When I was sad I had been able to bury my face in his soft, white fur. What should I do now with all this sadness?

'What do you say, Simone?' said Ingvar.

'I'm sorry,' I said.

And I was, too. I knew that he would be disappointed. He probably thought I would rush up and give him a hug of pure happiness. I was sorry he couldn't make me happy. He'd done his best. He had kept good face, even though for my sake he had crashed into his neighbour's beehives and dinged the nerdy car he adored. He had bought me a dog even though he really hated dogs – I knew that. He had done his best, and was sorry that I was sad.

'What did you say?' he asked, surprised.

'I'm sorry, Ingvar,' I said.

But he didn't understand. I knew that he never would. He giggled in a confused way at Mum. Grandpa blinked at me to show that he understood, at least. Except I knew he would.

Then the puppy came out from its hiding place. Its paws slipped on the floor. It rolled around and stopped with its nose trembling. But it couldn't smell anything familiar. Everything smelt dangerous and strange. So it set off again, slipped on one of Mum's screwed up balls of paper and cannoned towards a bottle of ink that splattered black blots around but for some unknown reason ended upright again. Mum grabbed one of the loose folds of skin as it skittled past her.

She lifted it into her lap. It lay there at peace, with its head against her breast. Mum stroked it slowly over its bubbly coat till it started to breathe calmly and was still and gave a satisfied little woof.

And I felt that I would also like to lie there. Why couldn't I creep into Mum's lap with the smell of perfume and tobacco, and let her stroke my forehead while I told her how impossible everything was, until it started to ease and nothing seemed so impossible anymore?

I went over to Mum and bent down and patted the dog as well. It sucked one of my fingers as if it was a nipple.

'I'm sorry I can't keep you, little puppy,' I said. 'I have to wait till my own dog comes home, do you see? And you're surely missing your mother.'

'But don't you understand?' said Ingvar. 'Kilroy is not coming back. He has disappeared. I've rung the police, and I've put in an ad. But he's nowhere to be found. That's just how it is. What's wrong with this little dog, eh? Isn't he cute?'

'There's nothing wrong with this dog,' I said and carried on stroking its velvety nose. 'It's really cute. It's just that it's not Kilroy. By the way, I know he's alive. I saw him myself.'

'Where?' said Mum.

'At Hötorget,' I said.

'That was most likely another dog,' said Ingvar. 'Can't you keep this one now? I bought him for you especially.'

'No,' I said, even though Ingvar sounded so disappointed.

Mum got up. She had the dog under one arm. She took hold of Ingvar with the other.

'Come on darling, we'll take this cute little baggage back to where you bought it,' she said. 'We'll leave these two grumpy old sticks and go for a ride in the car, just the two of us.'

'In that case, it will have to be in a taxi,' said Ingvar crossly.

Night came finally on that day, too. The stars shone wanly in the mist between dark floating clouds. Mum and Ingvar hadn't come back. They were probably trying to comfort each other. Mum, because she didn't know what to do about the magazine illustration on the joy of life. Ingvar, because he had failed to make me feel better. I couldn't sleep, and I knew that soon I would have to get up again.

I went up to Grandpa in what should have been my room. We lay beside each other and looked out at the sky. Grandpa had shifted the bed so it stood in the middle of the floor with its foot towards the window. The room was dark and our heads were raised with pillows. Together we glided through the endless universe, the eternal, quiet landscape of star clusters, planets and darkness. He kept his hand around mine.

'Why is everything like it is? Will it never end?' I whispered.

I had told him everything that had happened since the ill wind had blown into me: how I had been mistaken for a boy, about Isaac, how I had almost gone to jail for stealing a handbag, about the Bun and the Dove, and Kati's kiss. Grandpa cackled and clucked, a waterfall of laughter which made me laugh too, even though everything was so sad and confused and tiresome. Finally he had to dry his eyes with the sheet. And my eyes were wet too. In the end I didn't know if we were laughing or crying or both.

'You funny little thing,' he said and hugged me and gave me a smacking kiss on each cheek.

'Can't I make it stop?' I said.

'I think the small demons are playing games with you,' he said.

He sounded like he did when I was little, when I didn't know if he was joking or serious.

'Do they come from the devil?' I whispered.

'No, you ninny,' Grandpa whispered back. 'Do you know, if there was someone who created this whole fantastic universe with its suns and snails and flowers and people, then it wasn't just any boring old fart. It was more likely a godlike fruitloop, a heavenly nutcase full of suggestions, ideas and craziness. If it just so happened that in his haste he managed to create a kingdom where everything was good and clean and tidy and there was nothing there to change, then out of boredom he would have to go, tit for tat, looking for a little adventure. That's when he takes the form of small mischievous demons who stir things up and make nuisances and mischief down in the people's kingdom, so it won't be too boring to live here and so he can have some funny stories to tell back up in heaven.'

He was teasing me. I knew it. But still, I couldn't help feeling almost happy. I leaned against him. After a while he began to snore his soft, cello-like snore. I thought that he was the closest thing to a saint anyone could be.

I stroked him softly on the cheek before I left.

My night was not yet ended.

eighth chapter

I climb on the roof, make sure Isaac gets his birds, there is confusion and tumult in the classroom and the Bun is floored

It was either late night or early morning. Now and then, the moon peeped out from between its dark violet curtains and lit up the pearl necklaces hanging from strands of grass, buds and newly opened leaves. From the motorway, invisible trucks rumbled like giant bumblebees. Otherwise, it was quiet, although I could hear the lake water swishing its long skirts against the bridge's steel trouser legs in an endless, billowing dance.

That's the strange thing about those dark, quiet hours. They make you move your body carefully, softly and sneakily, like cats in trees. I breathed in the chilly air. I had Ingvar's fishing net over one shoulder and, in my Salomon rucksack, a packet of Wasa Fibre crackers and Ingvar's five-man tent bag. In the rose bush outside the classroom, a speckled cat lay with dew-drops on its whiskers, waiting for the right moment to catch the small birds off their guard. We each had the same goal, and I carried on without disturbing the cat.

Our classroom was highest up, on the third floor. I looked up to see if the window was still unlatched. Otherwise I wasn't really sure what I could do. I thought

I could see the wad of paper gleaming in the middle window, but I wasn't certain.

On the other side of the building was a fire escape. I managed to get myself up onto the bottom rung, by the skin of my teeth. Then all I had to do was climb. I left my rucksack and the fish net on the ground. The torch was in my back pocket. It was no trouble to get up onto the eaves. I sat astride the tiles on the roof, which felt cold and wet through my trousers.

From here I could see all around the wasteland we'd moved to: the lake, lying like a pool of spilt ink; the apartment blocks with lights still shining in some windows; new houses, and old summer houses with glass verandas from the time when all this was still countryside; and the zigzag outlines of fir trees on the far side. I wished we'd never moved here!

Then I started to climb down the roof. It wasn't very steep. I hoped I would be able to brake using my rubber soles and the palms of my hands. I was counting on coming down on the gutter right above our classroom window.

Suddenly, I felt my shoes losing their grip in the damp.

I was going to fall. Thunk, right onto the asphalt below! But then, with a squeak, my shoes found their grip again. When I'd got the whole way down, all I had to do was to get myself in through the window.

I sprawled out along the gutter and leaned carefully over the edge. My hands hurt after their journey down the roof. Jeepers, it was a long way down! I stretched out my right hand carefully and tried to open the window with the tips of my fingers. I was almost getting cramp in my left hand, which was hanging on to the gutter. The gutter didn't feel very solid. Finally, I managed to prise the window open with my fingernails.

Now all I had to do was get inside! I was sorry I hadn't taken Ingvar's lifeline with me as well. I crawled over the edge with my fingers gripping the gutter. For a moment I was hanging free. I couldn't reach the window ledge with my feet. To get myself in the window I had to swing in at speed with my legs, at the same time letting go with my hands. I could feel the distance to the ground as a tingling numbness in the soles of my feet.

Swish! My bum shot in the window and my back scraped against the window ledge as I dropped onto the gravy-brown cork floor. I leaned on a desk, while I got my breath back. The classroom looked strange in the dark. I turned on my torch and shone it around. Isaac's painting was hanging over there. Maybe I could try to get hold of a black swan. But there probably wouldn't be any brown ones. I turned the torch off again. I didn't want to let anyone know I was there if I didn't need to.

I went out to the corridor and down the steps.

I unlocked the big outside door.

There. Now all I had to do was to gather up a few birds.

The fat, comfortable ducks were dozing about the place, in the weeds around the schoolyard and the reeds at the edge of the lake. They had pushed their beaks into their side pockets and looked like a collection of black and brown boulders.

Catching them was about as hard as digging up potatoes. They'd been living on school food, clogging up their stomachs like blocked drains. Their instinct to flee had been overtaken long ago by fish balls, blood pudding, pieces of liver and blackhead-like lumps of potato.

All I had to do was pick them up.

I used the net like a spade and fished up the speckled-brown creatures. Then I popped them into the tent bag that was nice and roomy. Sharp, stern, quack-quacking sounds could be heard from the sack. Wide awake and confused, the rest of the birds popped out their heads and flapped their wings. Unused to all this, they started to waddle away on their skinny legs. They looked like the small fat joggers you saw on the running track at the rubbish tip.

The ducks woke the nearby pigeons. They clattered away, beating their wings against the night sky, which encouraged some gulls to screech over the schoolyard to see what was happening.

Initially I had planned on taking a couple of ducks. That should do it for Isaac. But I got carried away in a sort of mad intoxication. I popped one bird after another into the bag.

There was quacking and cackling, flapping and squawking from the full tent bag when at last I heaved it up the school steps. It was heavy and made me sweat.

I crushed the packet of Wasa Fibre crackers with my foot and sprinkled the contents over the classroom floor. That ought to be enough to keep them happy till school started. I untied the tent bag and shook out the screeching birds. Then I closed the door on them and went home to get a few hours' sleep.

From the stairs I could still hear their wild cackling. But they would calm down in a bit, I thought, very pleased with myself.

I came to school out of breath, fuzzy from lack of sleep and in a wonderful mood. It was late and I took the stairs in a few brisk steps.

The others were all standing outside the classroom door.

Kati sent me a magnificent smile and, quick as a wink, made her mouth into something that was supposed to resemble a kiss.

Isaac was looking crestfallen by the coat hangers. He probably didn't think I'd got the birds, so he was worrying about what the Bun was going to say.

I went up to him, giving Kati a little pat as I went past.

'I got the birds,' I whispered.

'I know,' he said, without enthusiasm.

'Brown,' I said.

'I know,' he mumbled, as if he was chewing on something he couldn't swallow.

'Ducks,' I said, winking to put him in a better mood.

But his face didn't change a bit. His mouth was forming up a new 'I know', but at that moment the Bun appeared and sort of gathered up our voices with her sweeping, white dress.

'What's this?' she cooed. 'Why are you all standing out here? Come on! In you go!'

She spread out her arms like a beautiful swan. Then I was suddenly aware of the noise. It came from inside the classroom: a wild, indescribable and heart-wrenching jangling noise.

That's why no one had gone in. They must have opened the door and then quickly shut it again. Eek!

I slowly began to understand that I had gone overboard. Five ducks would have been more than enough.

'Why won't you open up?' called the Bun, wrenching open the door.

She stopped on the threshold. Her mouth stayed open. And the loose flap of skin under her chin started to tremble like a frog's.

At least fifteen ducks were flapping and hopping and waddling around inside. The floor was covered in a layer of crackling breadcrumbs and bird poo; it was whirling about in the draught from the flapping wings. The birds turned their heads and looked at us sideways, each one with a hate-filled eye.

One of them tried to make a getaway. It travelled low with wings outstretched towards the doorway. Passing Bun's left ear, it shrieked. She raised her arms and wobbled on shaky high heels into the classroom.

Then she sat down with her back to the piano and put her hands over her face.

'Oh my goodness. Oh my goodness,' she said.

The first bird had already reached the hallway to the stairs. It was crashing from one wall to the other, madly squawking at its own echo. Two others took off from the back row of desks. With heavy wings, they came flapping over like a pair of volleyballs. But we were already inside and Frida had closed the door. At the last second they avoided the wooden door, did a clumsy starboard turn, and made an emergency landing on the lectern.

Kati beamed at me and poked out her tongue so I could see the red mark from my teeth. She picked up a duck and held it round the neck, just below the head, so it couldn't nip her.

'Open th'window!' she slurred at me with her sore tongue.

Then we all helped get rid of the birds. We hunted the hissing, shrieking, nipping beasts over the floor and desks. One by one, we heaved them out through the window, so they sailed down to the yard where the caretaker was standing with his mouth gaping. The last duck had flown up to one of the light shades. Fish and Stefan bombarded it with pieces of chalk till it cast itself off through the window of its own accord, terror in its eyes.

With the last duck gone, the room was uncomfortably quiet. The lamp in the ceiling still swayed as if from an invisible wind. It cast a weak light over the upside-down desks which lay amid heaps of writing blocks and schoolbooks; chairs leaning mournfully against each other; and the floor, with its crunchy coating of breadcrumbs, trampled bits of chalk, bird poo and pieces of paper.

The Bun sat in the midst of the devastation like a grown-up doll in a white lace dress. She sat in complete silence, legs stretched out, her back still to the piano. She didn't move. If her eyes weren't open, you would have thought she was asleep. Those big, white, beautiful hands rested together on her stomach. It was very spooky.

'They've gone now, miss,' Nettie said finally.

But she didn't answer.

Her fine nostrils flared, as if they wanted to take her

nose and fly it out through the window. I felt really bad. She had the same sad expression on her face that I'd seen on Mum's, after some extra-special party when the last guests had gone home and she was left alone with the dawn and a cloud of cigarette smoke. But that was a long time ago now.

None of us knew what to do.

'It's over now,' we said.

But still she didn't answer.

Carefully, as if we were afraid to wake someone, we carried the chairs and desks back to their normal places. Clever Pepsi was poking the blackboard cleaner with the pointer, using it to sweep the floor.

'What was the point of all this, then?' the Bun suddenly said, from her place on the floor.

We all jumped. We'd got used to the silence.

'It was me,' I said.

'What?' she said.

'Who brought them here,' I said. 'But that wasn't the idea.'

'What wasn't the idea?'

'That there should be so many. It just happened.'

'I see,' she said.

'But it was my fault really!'

That was Isaac. He stood so close to me that his blond mop was almost in my face.

'They were my birds,' he said.

'They were yours?' asked the Bun.

'Well, at least, not these ones exactly,' said Isaac. 'I didn't have any. And I was supposed to bring my birds with me today, the ones I don't have. And then I asked Simon, so he brought these ones.'

The Bun looked confused. A ray of sunlight made its way through the window and shimmered in Isaac's hair. I felt a sudden urge to take him by the shoulders and turn him around. But just then he turned and looked me straight in the eyes, so I had to quickly look away out the window.

'No, now I want you all to leave,' said the Bun tiredly, waving at the others. 'I want to be alone for a moment with Simon.'

The others disappeared. Isaac too. But before she left Kati crept up and gave me a friendly pat on the bum.

'Kithh-kithh, thhweetheart,' she slur-whispered in my ear.

So that left the Bun and me alone.

'Sit down,' she said.

I sat on the floor in front of her. Then it was quiet.

She looked at me with her large, sad eyes. We sat there without saying anything. Chalk dust fell softly in a light powder over us both. Time became eternal, as she kept quiet and I didn't know what to say. My saliva got stuck in my throat while her eyes swept over me like melancholy beams of light. I felt I couldn't stand it anymore. But still it went on.

'As you will understand, I'll have to speak to your parents,' she said at last. 'Mr Dove spoke to me yesterday about what you were doing in the girls' changing room. Not good. Then there was the cheating. In the few days you have been here you have caused more trouble than I have seen in many years. My-oh-my.'

Then I was allowed to go.

But she was coming home to talk to Mum. Things were getting worse, as they say. My-oh-my.

ninth chapter

The Bun meets a sourpuss, Mum is visited by a false model, Ingvar puts two and two together and there is a thunderstorm

She arrived at four o'clock.

She came up the hill at a snail's pace, wearing a light coat and carrying a flowery umbrella. Now and then she looked up at the sky where fantastic black clouds were gathering like fat, dark uncles at a funeral.

I saw her a long way off from my uncomfortable hiding place in a juniper bush. I had been there a long time and my feet were frozen. I had decided to secretly hear what was said at her home visit. I might be forced to step in.

She hesitated outside our gate and looked at our falling-down house, outside which Ingvar had parked his crumpled Fiat.

Then she caught sight of Axelsson through the hole in the hedge. He was in the process of nailing the roof back on to one of his scalped beehives.

'Excuse me!' she called.

'Whassat?' Axelsson called back, and he stopped hammering.

'I'm sorry, can you tell me if the Kroll family live in the house next to you?' the Bun screamed.

'Are you from the hospital?' the old man asked.

'What hospital?' The Bun sounded surprised.

'Have you come to get that crazy old man?'

'What crazy old man?' Now she was even more surprised.

'The one that turned up here a few days ago. D'ya know what he was wearing? Black ladies' boots and long-johns, eh! Stood and knocked on their door at six o'clock in the morning, eh!' said Axelsson, going redder in the face. 'Plays double bass at night!'

'I'm sorry, I'm here on another matter,' said the Bun, straightening the white dress which, truth be told, had some similarity to a nurse's uniform. She shook the umbrella as if it was a thermometer, ready to use.

'Then you must be from the insurance company, eh?' said Axelsson, as if this was a sort of game show, and he grabbed hold of the Bun's light coat with his dirty hands.

'My purpose …' she began.

'You're here to look at the trouble he's caused, eh?'

'The old man?' the Bun asked politely.

'No, no. Him, the serious one with the hat. That lives with the daughter of the old man.'

'What has he done?' Now the Bun's tone was conversational.

'What's he done?' Axelsson exploded. 'He's played tanks in my garden with his bloody car! First, straight through that hole in the hedge, a few skids here and there on the lawn, then he mows down my beehives! The devil! But I'll get him yet!'

He tried to drag the Bun in so she could see for herself what Ingvar had done to the garden, and to the beehives and the stairs to the house.

'I'm sorry.' She was snagged on some broken sticks in the hedge. 'I'm not from the insurance company.'

Axelsson frowned deeply. But then his face lit up.

'The boy!' he shouted. 'You're here for the boy!'

The Bun nodded, surprised at Axelsson's cleverness. I could feel my feet turning to ice.

'You've come to get him, eh?' said the old man happily. 'Yah, yah! That's what happens when you steal a handbag from an old lady! I saw it with my own eyes! They should come and get the whole lot of 'em, mark my words. Complete madhouse, I must say!'

'Stealing handbags,' the Bun sighed to herself.

'Stealing handbags, yah,' Axelsson repeated with expression. 'And so drunk he couldn't stand on his own two feet. Yah, yah. Is that what they teach them in school these days? Soon one of 'em will give me a karate chop in the head that kills me, eh? Ain't that so, little lady?'

The unusually large little lady shook her grown-up little head and took a couple of steps back with her mighty small feet.

She clearly didn't like the bit about school.

'Well, I must be going,' she said shortly. 'Thank you for the information.'

She went towards our house. She stood there, going up and down on her toes, and looked indecisive. Maybe she didn't dare go inside after all that Axelsson had come out with. I could always hope. If she still decided to hop into the hornets' nest, I could say my goodbyes. Everything would get found out. I might as well go and put on a dress directly! It would be the end of my disgraceful life as a boy.

As she stepped in through the gate, I rushed over the street, through the hole in Axelsson's hedge, criss-crossed his garden, jumped the fence and slid in through the open window to our house. I was going so fast that I almost put my head in a gigantic pot of simmering beetroot soup. At that moment, the door bell rang.

Things began magnificently.

From my vantage point behind the kitchen door, I could see the Bun's confused face when Mum opened the door. She stepped back so her heels were poised like a nervous diver's over the edge of the top step. Her cherry-red lips opened on something which might have been 'hello' if she hadn't had to stop for air at that very moment.

It sounded like, 'Huuuuaahh!'

'Welcome, dear friend. Wonderful! Fantastic that you could get here so soon!' Mum announced, and she took the Bun's coat sleeve and dragged her into the hall as if she was leading a horse into a stable. 'We'll take the coat off here, sweetie!' She pulled off the Bun's fur-collared coat with a single elegant gesture.

When Mum turned in my direction I understood why the Bun looked so perturbed. Mum was wearing a worn-out jacket of fire-red silk velvet with embroidered gold dragons and paint flecks on it. Underneath she had a pair of shocking-pink ballet tights and Mexican felt boots. These clothes were relatively normal for Mum. However her face looked a bit strange. She had coated it with yoghurt, yeast and sticky egg white, according to a recipe she had found in one of the ladies' magazines she illustrated.

With her long, crow-black hair she looked like a barbarian who had won first prize for the Most Terrible Dance Mask.

Mum took the Bun by the arm and led her happily into the sitting room which was bathed in light from the chandelier, because the cloud had pulled black blinds across the sun.

'This is Ingvar!' she said, sweeping out her arm. 'He's not professional either,' she added informatively.

He didn't look very professional.

He was sitting in a pus-green steel bath at the far end of the room. The frozen kneecaps of his white, knobbly legs stuck out of water which also held plastic ducks, a whale spitting a fountain from a hole in its back, and a sail boat. A little wind-up swimmer buzzed around the edge.

There were a lot of other toys in an open black briefcase on the floor.

'Nice to meet you.' Ingvar raised his hat with a shy smile.

He straightened his impeccable tie and sober blue blazer.

'And this is my father!' Mum continued to introduce the family.

Grandpa sat in his rocking chair with a small smile on his face.

He nodded easily to the Bun.

Mum had gone back to turning the surprised, mute Bun around and around like a carousel of white material and rosy skin.

'Wonderful!' Mum burst forth. 'Exactly what I was looking for! What a beautiful, full body! Don't you think?' She patted the confused woman on the tummy.

She led the Bun to the sideboard which was set up behind the bath. It had been transformed into a coffee table, covered with cream-cakes, pieces of tart, friands, biscuits, vanilla hearts and Danish pastries.

'Take a seat,' said Mum, pulling over a chair beside the table. 'That's it. Very good. With your elbow on the table and the cigarette holder in your mouth. Very good. You look really cute, all of you!'

My stomach was turning upside down. The pungent smell of beetroot soup was in my nose. I wanted to rush from my hiding place and free the Bun from Mum who was in the middle of painting highlights and drawing lines on her terrified face so she'd look like an old film vamp. For her head she was given the same wide-brimmed hat Ingvar had worn a few days ago.

She sat there and didn't know what to say. When Mum was like this, you could get overwhelmed; all you could do was to go with it, like on a swelling sea.

'I'm sorry if I'm rushing you,' said Mum, from the drawing board. 'But this has to be finished on the dot! Always these damn deadlines!'

She worked with her pens and paintbrushes like one possessed. Ingvar was already caught on paper with a playful smile on his face. Now the Bun rose off the white like an over-fertile, flirting angel in a playground of marzipan, chocolate and small cloud puffs of cream.

'The joy of life, that's it!' Mum said. 'A picture of joy. This is a picture of love, plenty, colour, lust, playfulness and craziness. Don't you think? Of course it is.'

She was talking to herself.

I started to understand what had happened. She had been waiting for someone who would sit as a model for her picture of the joy of life. And then the Bun had appeared.

The Bun took the cigarette holder from her mouth. She was clearly trying to gather herself together.

'This is a mistake,' she said in a thin voice.

'Mistake!' Mum said strongly. 'Do you think this is a mistake, darling? These days we are supposed to hate having fun. That's the latest. You have to torture yourself to enjoy yourself. Dieting, jogging, fasting, sweating, stretching, running, rushing! How I hate it!'

'That wasn't what I meant,' said the Bun. 'I am Miss …'

'And so am I!' Mum butted in. 'But what does it matter, Miss or Mrs? You still have the same right to have fun. Isn't that true?'

The Bun looked about to give up. She absentmindedly poked her finger into one of the sticky cream-cakes and sucked the fluffy lick of cream.

'It's about the boy,' she began again, with a look of suffering in her eyes. 'It's been a problem for the last while, you understand. In school. He's caused a lot of, how shall I put it, mischief.'

'Oh,' said Mum. 'That is sad to hear. It isn't anything serious, I hope.'

What should I do now? Outside the air started to rumble, deep and threatening, as if echoing how I was feeling. The sky was completely black to the horizon. Our house was like a tiny, lit-up dollshouse in a dark room. Should I creep over to Grandpa and ask him to help, without anyone seeing me? He could pretend to be senile and chase the Bun out of the house. But it was probably too late. And anyway he seemed to have fallen asleep in his rocking chair.

'I don't know. Maybe not,' said the Bun. 'But it has become too much. I don't really know what to do with him …'

'Well, I'm not an expert,' said Mum.

'Who is?' said the Bun. 'But you still need to talk …'

'Of course,' said Mum. 'What has the little beggar been up to then? Talk away. I am the perfect ear, dear.'

While the Bun slowly and painfully started to explain all the trouble I had been in, the thunder came closer and closer. Mum said 'Mmm' and 'Aahh' and swept a glittering sheen of colour over the picture with her brush. Ingvar swayed amongst brilliant green, pink and white, the Bun and the toys and baking against a blue-grey background.

Now the surprise, I thought, looking at Mum. But her face gave away nothing.

'Well, that's how it is,' the Bun concluded her terrible list of outrage.

'Do you know,' said Mum, ripping off the picture and waving it a little so it could dry. 'I've really listened to what you've said and it sounds quite a lot.'

She wiped off the muck from her face with a rag she dipped into Ingvar's bath water.

'Are you done now?' Ingvar took the opportunity to ask. 'I'll get cystitis if I sit any longer in this cold water.'

'Is that all you've got to say?' The Bun sounded anxious.

Mum was already pulling on her gumboots.

Was she so upset she was just going to leave?

'You'll have to excuse me,' she said. 'But as I said,

I'm in a bit of a hurry. It was really kind of you to come along. And as for everything you've been telling me about your son, I think you should be proud of him in some ways. He seems incredibly full of life and imagination!'

'My son,' the Bun hiccupped.

'That's the one,' said Mum. 'And do you know what, you shouldn't worry about all that business with the clothes. My daughter dresses just the same.'

Then she was out the door.

The Bun looked as if she was out the door too. She raised herself up out of the chair and went to the front door, still wearing the hat and the wonderful eye shadow. Ingvar slopped over there as well, dripping water from his sopping blazer. With the face of a waiter who has lost his trousers, he helped the Bun into her coat.

'She didn't understand it was her son I was talking about!' said the Bun.

'I'm sorry,' said Ingvar, 'but she doesn't have a son.'

Then the Bun glided out the door, out into the darkness, the noise and the pelting rain.

Saved by the bell. Dong!

The sky flared and flashed with lightning. The earth trembled from the thunder as if the clouds were enormous stones grating together. The rain poured down and clothes were wet through in an instant. I had slipped out through the kitchen window again so I could get wet. Otherwise Ingvar would guess that I had been inside.

While I stood outside I saw a woman in white go sailing up our stairs. It was the real model. She trotted back down again after a moment looking very cross. What had Ingvar said to her?

I breathed out. Those demons Grandpa told me about were doing a really good job! But how long would everything hold together? Had Mum really got everything round the wrong way? It did seem possible.

When I came in, Ingvar sat in the rocking chair. Grandpa had gone somewhere else.

'Hi!' I said. 'Have you been out in the rain with those legs?'

'Ehh,' he huffed, stuffing his pipe which smelt as if he had filled it with crumbled rubber soles.

'Where's Mum?' I asked.

'Gone to the magazine with a picture,' said Ingvar. 'She'll be back soon.'

'Grandpa then?'

'Upstairs resting.'

After that I couldn't think of anything else to say. I went over to the window. The black boulders had come down to roof level. They were tumbling around harder and harder as if in a gigantic rock crusher, sending squalls of sparks shooting about like welding flames. The storm was on top of us now!

I leaned my forehead against the cold pane and thought about how Mum had said that the Bun could be really proud of the son she didn't have, 'so full of life and imagination' or whatever it was. She would never say that about me! I started to relax at last. I had done it!

'You can stop it now!' said Ingvar.

'What?'

'I know all about it. No point in trying to get out of it,' he continued, in a sinister voice.

Dong! The whole house seemed to shake. When I turned around, Ingvar's face was lit up by lightning.

It looked white and nasty. My head started spinning. What did he mean, 'all about it'? Of course, the idiot had sat in the bathtub and heard the Bun and worked out that the son was me! I had almost forgotten about him. Someone should have pushed his head under the water! Now he would take me off to school and drag off my boy clothes and I'd have to stand there like an idiot and be laughed at forever! It was all his fault! He had started everything!

'What I don't understand is why? Why in heaven's name?' he said.

He had got up and was coming towards me.

He wouldn't catch me!

'Simone!' he called out.

But by then I was already at the outside door. I heard his damp footsteps behind me.

The lights were on at Axelsson's. Now he'd get a few more spiffy details to tell everyone about his neighbours, since Ingvar was crashing through the doorway in his undies with bare legs, wearing a blazer, with an absurd little hat on top of his head.

I ran off towards the rubbish tip. With lightning switching on and off, it was like being continuously photographed with a flash. I heard Ingvar coming closer. My legs felt heavy. The rain shrank my tight jeans so that they rubbed with every step. Ingvar had an advantage over me. He would catch up to me.

Then I noticed an oak tree that stretched its gnarly limbs to the sky. It wouldn't be hard to climb! With a jump, I reached the lower branches and pulled myself up. With arms and legs that had practised on hundreds of trees, I climbed higher and higher, right up to the top where the branches thinned out. This would be too much for Ingvar's fear of heights!

He was below me already.

'Come down, for God's sake!' he yelled, trying to drown out the thunder.

Everything ran together. Rain burned my ears. Thunder blasted me in the chest. The ground was mixed with the sky into a single haze, dappled with flares of lightning. It was as if I was in an endless sea where the light didn't have the energy to reach the whole way down.

'Never!' I yelled back.

'It's dangerous, you stupid idiot!' he screamed.

'I don't give a rat's arse!' I screamed, and the words made my mouth taste like vinegar.

'You're completely nuts!' he called as if he wanted to cry.

'If you want to catch me, then come on up!' I hollered.

I saw him grab hold of the same branch that I had climbed up on. Clumsily, he grabbed it with his legs and managed to crawl up to the next branch. I thought I could see his terrified eyes. Unsteadily, he scrambled up the trunk, his feet edging up the slippery branches. Slowly he came higher up. With every branch he managed, I was sure he would fall.

'Stop!' I called out. 'You'll fall!'

But he didn't stop. He fought his way upwards.

'Son of a devil!' he cried.

At that moment the sky caught fire. It exploded with a terrible crack. It crashed over us like a burning roof in a fever of hot flames. Blinded, I grabbed hold of the branch with my legs and arms. It felt like it was being wrenched from my grip.

The air pricked my nostrils. I could see that the rubbish tip was burning. I was sure the lightning had struck our tree. Below me, Ingvar hung upside down. His hat had fallen to the ground. At any moment he would also plummet from the sky.

Suddenly I understood that he had climbed up to save me. Even though he was a stupid hat idiot and a dipstick, I couldn't let him break his neck.

'Help! For God's sake, will you try to help me,' he begged.

When I got down to about his level I could see the terror of death in his eyes. His face was as white as one of the Bun's dresses.

'You say nothing, right?' I said. 'Nothing about what you know.'

He shook his head.

'You understand, it has to run its course. Telling would only make things worse. Do you understand?'

He continued to shake his head.

'Do you have to kiss girls though?' he wondered stupidly.

I shook my head.

'Can you help me get down now?' he asked.

I nodded and patted him on his wet, almost hairless skull.

I managed to get him facing the right way up again. Then I climbed past him and put his feet on the branches I thought would carry him. His legs felt stiff and cold.

Everything went well until there were only a few branches left. Then, swish, Ingvar fell past me and out of the tree. It wasn't terribly high, so I thought he would be all right. But when I came down he was having trouble standing on his foot. He had to hold me round the shoulders as we made our way home.

'I'm sorry,' I said.

'It's okay,' he said.

'Where have you been?' Mum asked when we got home.

She looked at Ingvar's scratched, bare legs and his ruined blazer.

'Out climbing trees,' Ingvar said with a grin.

'Lordy, what a pair of idiots!' Mum rolled her eyes.

Then we sat down and ate beetroot soup with sour cream and warm bread. And Mum was in a really good mood, like she always was when she had finished a painting. We laughed. And Ingvar's leg swelled up round the ankle so that his whole foot looked like a beetroot. Otherwise he looked unusually un-nerdlike.

'I think it's best we take that to the hospital,' Mum said when we had finished our coffee.

tenth chapter

Grandpa visits a falling-down house, he plays the cello for the last time and the gulls sing in joy and in sorrow

The rain continued. The whole night it clattered on the roof. It continued all the next day, Saturday. I lay in the mahogany monster with the covers over my ears and enjoyed the storm drumming against the window panes, the wind in the tops of the trees outside, the cold and the foul weather. Mum baked bread and it smelt of fennel and aniseed. Ingvar sat with his leg outstretched and his foot in plaster. He filled in insurance forms and whistled happily to the weather report which promised continued rain and prolonged wind and cold. Grandpa kept them company in the kitchen, reading cookbooks which smelt of dust and grease, stroking his nose while the clocks chimed.

Nothing happened and it was wonderful. The demons were clearly taking a break. They probably needed a rest. Them too.

The only thing that disturbed the peace was when Kati rang. She slurred and cooed into the phone and invited me to a party on Monday and asked if I wanted to go to a movie with her. I said yes to the party and no to the movie. She sounded cross and said she would ask Isaac instead. I pictured how she would sit and slur with that pointy tongue in his ruffled hair. Bugger!

I went out to the kitchen to drown the tingling in my stomach with a 7 Up and some old cheese doodles. Grandpa took a break from his long list of recipes. He gazed out at the tempestuous weather outside.

'Tomorrow, my wee darlings, it will be a beautiful sunny day,' he said in a sing-song voice, 'and we'll go on a trip to the country.'

'Ha ha,' answered the rain on the windows.

Something was stroking me lightly on the cheek. I glimpsed a freckled face.

'Uppity-up, my small dove,' he sang in my ear. 'Look how the sun's shining!'

His white moustache was tickling me. And his eyes shone clear and blue as fjords and inlets and oceans. I forgot my crossness about being woken and dragged away from my dreams. Grandpa clucked like wavelets and the curtains were swept by a warm breeze.

'You must help me get ready, my child,' he said.

Sure.

I traipsed up to the attic and rummaged in all the boxes we had put away. I managed to find most of what he wanted: his walking stick with a silver handle shaped like a wolf's head, the cream felt hat with the floppy brim, his summer suit of white linen, a shirt with removable collar, and those wonderful white leather shoes with brown toe caps with tiny holes.

I sneaked around so I didn't wake the others, while Grandpa stood in his nightshirt, ironing away the wrinkles and folds of the suit with a piping-hot iron.

When we were finished I led him down to the bathtub in the basement. I was starting to get good at leading people around. I filled the tub with steaming hot water and Grandpa slipped in with a pleased look on his face. His skin was white and covered in small fine wrinkles. I scrubbed it carefully with tar soap that smelt of summer and childhood.

'Wonderful!' he breathed.

In a festive mood, we dressed him in one garment after another. It felt like putting the old Grandpa back together again; radiant, strong and big as a bear, he emerged from the rugs on the floor!

We made breakfast and packed the old picnic basket with chicken, sausage, cheese, bread, cucumbers, long-necked bottles and a thermos. We were just finished when Mum and Ingvar came down.

Mum stopped in the doorway with her eyes fastened on the stately figure in front of her.

'Father,' she said slowly.

She went up to him and touched him and patted him a little here and there.

'Dressed for summer?' she said.

'Yep, it's time now, my dear,' he said.

'Just like before,' Mum said.

'Just like before,' he said.

She got tears in her eyes. And she had to kiss his shiny bald head and both of his pink, clean-shaven cheeks.

'My goodness, you are stylish,' she giggled.

'Stop that idiocy right now!' Grandpa said sternly.

He smiled a shy sort of a smile with those crooked wolf teeth and fished his pocket watch up like a goldfish out of his vest pocket.

'Hurry up and eat,' he said. 'The wagon will be here at any moment.'

I was almost expecting a horse and carriage. But when it came it was a normal taxi.

At last we were on our way!

The castle disappeared like a mouldy cake behind us. The Grand Hotel was all lit up with rows of windows. And the whole town floated by, with its empty churches, houses and old people's homes, and crazy dreams of stones and marble.

We sat in the stern of the Sun Star ferry, Grandpa, Mum and me.

Ingvar hadn't come along. He was going to rest his lump of plaster. He also had a cold after all his hours sitting in the bathtub. But I think he wanted to leave us in peace. He had no memories of these trips. And he understood that we were making a journey back in time.

Grandpa sat in the wheelchair we had borrowed from the hospital, parked between a red Honda and cases of beer. Soon we were out in open waters. The sky stretched light blue and still and dripping in sun with gulls wafting around, dizzy from the light and the breeze. We passed bays, with ducks and swans and grebes and terns.

Grandpa pointed out islands and lighthouses and castles and said what their names were, as he had done so many times before. His eyes swept like a pair of birds over the countryside.

'Do you see?' he called, pointing with his stick at one thing after another. 'Do you see how beautiful it is?'

We nodded as we had always done.

'Pfft,' he said. 'You don't see at all. You're a couple of real chooks. Look there now. Olga, do you see!'

Mum gave a small smile and leaned her head against his.

I went inside, bought some car-shaped sweets with 'Sweden's most-popular cars' on the packet and looked at the people. Kids were sitting with shiny metal music players like yowling puppies in their laps. Old people leaned over their sandwiches and plastic-covered maps. Toddlers crawled around among banana peels and waste-paper baskets on the floor; from the cat baskets you could see avaricious, yellow eyes eyeing-up bird cages, and in the foyer was a chaos of suitcases, backpacks, tomato plants, rolls of tar paper, stern ropes and fridges. And I had thought we would be alone on the boat!

When I came back they were still sitting there the same as before. In the shadow of the felt hat I could see Grandpa's eyes. The blue water reflected in them and ran in steady streams down his cheeks. He didn't bother to wipe away the tears. He didn't even appear to notice them. In his arms he held the cello case. He had insisted that the cello came along.

'What's the matter?' I asked.

'What?' he said, as if he was deep in dreams.

'Why are you crying?'

'Bah!' he said and pinched me on the nose. 'For sorrow and gladness, I suppose. Because I'm old and crazy, of course. Why else? What else should your eyes do when they see all this beauty around us? Eh!'

He blew his nose noisily in a clean handkerchief.

'It's such a long time since we came out like this. And it's the first time without Katarina. Maybe it's that most of all, Miss Curiosity-in-a-cone! For longing and love for your grandmother! So now you know.'

Yes, Grandma had always been with us – small, plump, with her broad, friendly face, happy and laughing, and a Parisian hat on her head. When Grandpa got cross, which he did often, she just blew in his face.

With Katarina, the trips to the beloved island had also disappeared. Summers were never again magical and Grandpa never seemed as crazy and happy when he didn't have someone to blow in his face any more.

'I have to make this journey one more time, monkey. And I haven't had the courage to do it until now.'

He sniffed loudly so that people turned around and a middle-aged lady in a flowery dress appeared.

'Are you not feeling well, sir? Would you like a painkiller?' she asked.

She dug around in her handbag full of jars of pills, which rattled like a rattlesnake.

'I'll cry as much as I want to, you dried-up dipstick! Do you hear?' Grandpa shouted and he threatened her with his stick.

The lady drew back in fear.

Then I blew in Grandpa's face.

First he looked surprised. Then his face brightened just like that.

'You little witch,' he said warmly, stroking me on the cheek.

The house stood where it always had, for as long as I could remember, painted white, daft and festive with its tower-like extensions, its roof rack and balcony where Grandma would always stand and wave. It was on the top of a rocky knoll with a crooked gravel path leading up to it. 'Felix Kroll. Private' was written on a brass sign on the gate. Felix Kroll was Grandpa's father. He was the one who built the house.

We couldn't get any further than the overgrown alley of elm trees with the wheelchair. On the left was the fallen-down jetty. The ice had crushed it.

As we stood there, a swan came flying over the bay with its feet out like a pair of water-skis. Its wings were open, stretched to their full span, and its neck was thrust forwards. It blasted with a sound like an organ when it landed. I knew I had seen it before.

'We can go around the road instead,' Mum suggested.

'No,' said Grandpa. 'I know it sounds stupid. But I want to get up there myself.'

Painfully, he fought his way up the knoll. The sweat ran from his face and he breathed heavily while the sun turned in the sky among the gulls and curlews. It took more than an hour for him to get up to the house.

On shaking legs, with hat in hand, he finally stood outside the front door.

'I'm here now,' he said, as if he was talking to someone invisible.

We went quietly through the house. Everything was still the same as it had been that day five years ago when Grandma died and Grandpa locked the door. He went in the helicopter that took Grandma away. And then he never returned. It was as if he just closed the door on his sorrow.

The spiders had cobbled together lace curtains for the windows, and the flowers that Grandma looked after so carefully had dried out so their leaves drooped over their pots. On the dining-room table sat a soup pot where fragrant steam had been replaced by dust motes. The table was set for two. The wine had evaporated in the crystal glasses, leaving hard rings of red on the bottoms. Grandma's Parisian hat was hanging on one of the dining chairs with carved lion heads. Her shoes were helter-skelter beneath the sofa, kicked off in a hurry, like windblown boats cast up on the shore.

The grandfather clock in the corner had stopped.

Grandpa took the little lever from a shelf in the corner cupboard and wound it up. It started with a creaking sigh.

He went slowly around the room, stroking things as if to remind himself what they felt like. He straightened cloths and cushions, picked up a hair pin, and came to a standstill with the tiny thing in his fingers. He closed an open book on the writing desk, straightened the chairs, saw how the paintings of ships and oceans and islands in the two old ship cabinets had flaked and fallen to pieces, and saw how the wallpaper was streaked with damp.

Then he came to a standstill in front of the sofa.

Next to one of the armrests was an embroidered cushion. It was crumpled, with a dent in the middle, as if someone had recently rested their head on it.

Grandpa bent over and buried his face in it.

'I can still smell her perfume,' he said.

Then he took one of the kitchen chairs outside and sat on its edge with his cello between his knees. The light evening breeze tickled his white moustache. The sun shone mildly like a kerosene lamp hung in the evening sky over the fjord and the rocky knoll where we sat.

Slowly he set the bow against the strings. He played one of the pieces he had played when I was little, Bach's Sonata Number 2 for cello and piano. But now there was no piano. That's what Grandma had played. Now there was the quiet, the shriek of gulls, the quacking of ducks and the sound of the water. Grandpa closed his eyes and played and the notes rose mumbling and groaning, angry and tender, so that I could hear his voice in them. They spoke of his sorrow and his longing for the piano's dazzling smile and chubby, black body, and of his love for the stones, the rushes, the pines, the birds, the pale sky and the black earth.

Mum sat wearing Grandma's Parisian hat. I don't know what she was thinking about. But she took my hand where we sat beside each other on the rocks. I leaned on her shoulder. While the music continued its sorrowful tune I crept closer. It was a long time since we had sat like this, without arguing or fighting or annoying each other. And I had missed it. I didn't know if it was still possible. I had been moving away, learning how to be a fruitloop on my own. Mum shone and glittered and radiated so much that I almost disappeared, like stars do when the sun comes up. I held her hand and looked at Grandpa who was also going away.

Suddenly I saw Grandma sitting beside Grandpa. With her plump legs and broad feet and wise eyes she almost looked more real than Grandpa. She nudged his bald head with her round cheek. Grandpa smiled happily at his cello. Then she disappeared into the music, or wherever she'd come from.

Was a love like this possible anymore? I thought of Mum, of all the men who'd come and gone, barefoot or with creaking shoes, through our apartment. Maybe forever-love was dead – like mammoths, gas lights and gramophones?

And while the music sniffed and laughed, pictures of Kati and Isaac kept popping up. Was that what I felt for them? I saw Kati's yellow eyes and Isaac's blue ones, like Mum's and Grandpa's. What did they want from me? What did I have to do with them?

A heavenly laugh cackled from the dark wooden instrument.

Then it was over.

The final notes were as light as dandelion seeds floating over the heather, over the water, and rising towards the sky. Grandpa sat still for a moment with his bow in his hand and eyes shining. He looked tired out. Then he lifted the colossal cello high above his head and smashed it against the rocks.

'Its final song,' he said with a tired smile.

We lit the woodstove. Mum and I went to bed after a while. But Grandpa stayed sitting at the window. I could hear him padding around, pulling out drawers and opening cupboards while the grandfather clock ticked towards morning. When it came, he laid a floral silk dress on my bed.

'I want you to have this, my pigeon,' he said. 'Katarina was wearing this the first time we met.'

It was Sunday. We went home again at midday. Grandpa had cleaned and folded and aired. He was done. On the way down to the boat he didn't mind sitting in the wheelchair. He sat with the colossal samovar in his lap, like a shiny chimney. He wanted to take it with him.

We probably should have loaded it with coal and set it going. It had started to get cold again.

I was freezing.

eleventh chapter

In which I go to Kati's party, fall over Ingvar's shoes, get my ears boxed and challenge someone I love

I turned up late. First I thought about not going at all – which would have been a good idea. Instead I stole one of Ingvar's best shirts out of his wardrobe – white with pale-blue stripes – and a pair of his black shoes and off I went. The shirt and the shoes were both a couple of sizes too big. I stumbled off in the cold, still freezing, as I had been for the past twenty-four hours. The wind from the lake was really cold. It crept into the gap between my neck and collar and puffed me up so I looked like the Michelin Man sitting on top of a big truck.

When I arrived, the party was well under way.

The heat is on blasted from the loudspeakers, but I still felt cold. The room was packed with people my age. I stumbled over to the big windows in the enormous sitting room, with a diet Coke in one hand and a fistful of crumbling cheese doodles in the other. In the garden, the pool was lit up like an aquarium for winter swimmers. Further away was the real lake, unlit and black.

I stood behind the curtains and shoved my oversized clown feet into the shagpile carpet so that no one could see them. I shivered and thought about leaving again. No one had noticed me yet.

But something made me stay.

I looked around. What was I looking for? A gang of guys from somewhere north of town stood munching on a huge bowl of prawns. I could hear their posh *as* like sheep's baaing, squeezed out of their wingtip collars pulled together by skinny black ties. Otherwise I recognized most people. Fish and Dannie and Stefan were trying their best to consume the entire supply of soft drinks, chips, snacks and dips, peanuts, pretzels and jelly snakes. Ant and Para were stuffing themselves on the gold velvet sofa that looked like a huge cheese doodle. Frida and Nettie were hanging out on the edge of an empty circular space, which was probably meant for dancing. Pepsi seemed to be taking a floor lamp to pieces and putting it back together again.

Then I saw them.

Kati had her arms wrapped around his neck. I could see his soft blue eyes. He didn't see me. He was looking into Kati's white-powdered face, her black-painted eyes and fire-red lips. Her black nest of hair hid most of his face. The moment before I saw them, I had the feeling that someone was looking at me from their direction, but I must have been mistaken.

I went over, even though I knew I shouldn't. They didn't see or hear anything. I buried my face in the hair nest as well.

'How's your tongue, sweetie?' I asked.

'Oh, ishat shou?' she said. 'Ish shine. My shongue ish shine.'

'Good,' I said, feeling colder than ever. 'And how about you then?'

I turned to Isaac.

'What?' he said.

'Don't need any birds or anything?' I said with a frozen smile.

I felt the nastiness welling up inside me again.

'Are you jealous?' he said calmly.

That calm made me furious. I was ready to punch him. But he had already slipped out of Kati's arms and was on his way to the chips-and-snacks gang. That dizzying moment when I had thought I could see life flowing quietly like a stream, joy and sorrow melding together in the music of the cello, everything somehow merged together – that moment was long gone. I was right in the middle of it all again.

Jealous? Should I be jealous of him? There I was, standing there like a clown; dressed up as something I wasn't, getting hot looks from those sooty-black eyes while the person I really liked went off to eat jelly snakes. Very funny!

'Come on,' said Kati, pulling me away. 'We can carry on from where we left off.'

I stretched my neck and thought I caught a glimpse of Isaac's spiky hair while Kati transported me over the never-ending carpet with its pattern of trampled cheese doodles.

She hummed in my ear in her hoarse, purring voice:

Stay. I want you to stay ...
Make up your mind, decide.
We could be making love tonight
Tell me 'yes' and not 'I might' ...

Then I fell over those blasted shoes!

I grabbed hold of Kati with both hands and hobbled forwards. Whatever I did, the shoes got in the way, crossing each other, bending, and finally shoving their noses into the fringe of a rug like a pair of crashing jet planes.

We spun around the posh guys and fell into the table with the bowl of prawns on it.

It rolled away and collided with a potted South Pacific palm tree. We landed softly on the carpet, except I hit the table with my head and felt completely groggy. I lay on top of Kati with my arms still clamped around her body.

'Ousch!' she said. 'Do you hasch to be quite show dramashic?'

I tried to drag myself up. But the tablecloth had been pulled on top of us and the more I tried to get out the more I got tangled.

Kati's eyes were full of laughter.

I wanted to cry.

'What are you two doing down there on the floor?' said one of the snobby guys.

Kati gave me a kiss on the cheek.

'We can't justh lie here, scharling,' she said quietly.

'You're right there,' I said.

At last we got back to our feet. I saw grinning faces everywhere. I was furious and cold and I tried to smile back as well as I could. How long would this go on? Where was Kati planning on taking me?

At that moment Pepsi managed to get the floor lamp he'd been mucking around with working. It started to blink with hard, red flashes of light, transforming the empty floor space to a shimmering disco with Siouxie and the Banshees singing their hopeless songs right into our waiting ears.

'Come on,' said Kati, pulling me over there. 'Let's dance.'

How did boys dance? I figured this was probably one of those moments when you reveal yourself, in how you move. I tried to make my movements a little more edgy, imitating a nerdy, frozen Travolta who had just got a table in the head. I felt jealous of Kati hopping back and forth, light-footed, so her hair flew and her breasts swayed in that blouse that looked like a corset. She was probably trying to look like Jennifer Beals in *Flashdance*, the movie I hadn't seen, that she went to with Isaac.

If I were a boy I would love her.

If I were a boy I would lie in bed at night and think about her.

If I were a boy I would long for that pointy little tongue and those golden eyes.

If I were a boy, like Isaac, I thought – and then I went over on my ankle and it hurt so much I got tears in my eyes.

'I like you, Simon,' she sang when she came near me. 'No one else has thrown me around like a half kilo of cheese on the sitting room floor and then given me a hug and rolled me up in a tablecloth in the middle of a party!'

'It was a mistake,' I said. 'All this is a mistake! Do you hear? Can't you understand?'

'I don't understand anything,' she said with a smile.

'I like you too,' I said. 'But not like that.'

'Like what?' she called in my ear.

She snaked so close that her breasts stuck into Ingvar's poser-shirt and it felt like they were mine and the wad of cotton in my pants moved around a bit.

She thought it was a game, like biting tongues and rolling around among the prawns.

'I can't be your boyfriend!' I said and tried to make my voice as hard as the clump of ice in my stomach. 'There's no point!'

'What?' she said and I saw that she was starting to understand.

We stood quite still, still too close.

'It's not your fault,' I said. 'It's probably me there's something wrong with, I imagine.'

'What sort of wrong?' she said softly as if she wanted me to know what an excellent nurse she was.

'I'm just not attracted to you,' I said, to put a stop to it.

'Yes you are,' she said confidently.

'No. I promise,' I said idiotically.

'But the kiss? And the hugs? And … everything.'

'It just happened by mistake,' I said.

'You shit!'

She hit me. Then she left me alone among the people who were smiling and watching and whispering in the blinking pool of light.

I should have left then, if not before. I should have never come in the first place. But even though I had been idiotic enough to turn up, I should have had the sense to leave right then.

The rest of the party was a complete disaster.

I mostly stood and watched. I could feel Kati's aggrieved, sorrowful eyes on me, and I looked for Isaac. The loudspeakers blared louder, like black bomber planes over the messed-up carpet. Some people calling themselves Joyful Lackeys sang joyless songs about how tired they were of everything, tired of loving, tired of living. And we danced along. Kati danced with Isaac. They clung to each other as if they were also very tired.

I danced with Anna. Not because I wanted to dance, really, but because I wanted to be close to them. I led Anna and followed along in their footsteps to see if I could hear what they were saying. But I couldn't. Maybe they weren't talking at all. Maybe they were just keeping each other warm.

I was freezing. And Anna looked at me through her glasses which blinked red as well. She probably wondered what sort of dance I was trying to do. In honour of the evening she was dressed much like the stick insect she had at home. She was wearing a brown dress that looked like a sleeping bag sack. And brown shoes. And her hair was brown.

I kept standing on her feet. Not because I meant to. It was almost as if she put them there herself.

'Stop that!' she yelled so loudly that everyone turned around.

They thought I was trying to wrestle her to the floor or pinch her somewhere you shouldn't pinch! I felt my ears going red as if I really had done something bad.

'That guy can't keep his hands to himself,' I heard one of the snobby guys say.

I left the dance floor.

I stood in a corner and sulked.

After a while the doors to the garden opened. A cold wind swept in. Laughing, everyone went out with charcoal and sausages and lit a barbecue which looked like a cut-off sewage pipe. The coal glowed like fallen stars and it smelt of kerosene and burnt meat.

I scooted off with a sooty, sad-looking sausage which was calling to me with its skin broken, looking as sorry for itself as I felt.

Isaac and Kati sat in the green light of the pool.

Their feet were splashing in the ice-cold water. They sat close together, looking into each other's eyes. Why was I wearing these damned boy's clothes? It wasn't fair! I felt like shoving them both into the pool. I couldn't bear to see them!

'Are you going to swim?' I heard Fish ask.

'Too cold,' said Isaac.

'He doesn't dare!' I squawked so that everyone heard me.

It sounded stupid, I could tell. But what else could I say?

Isaac looked up.

'What's with you?' he said. 'Why are you hanging after us all the time? Can't you find something else to do?'

'You're just a big bluffer,' I said. 'Do you get that? Are you as good a swimmer as you say? You don't even dare get wet!'

Isaac was a competitive swimmer. His father was a swimming trainer. Everyone knew that. I don't know if he was what you'd call an 'Olympic hopeful'. But there were people who thought he would go a long way. I had never seen him swim, but I had heard people talking about it.

'Lay off, Simon!' said Isaac. 'If you really want, we can both jump in. It seems like you need to cool down a bit.'

I didn't have any desire to jump into that hole of a swimming pool. I was already freezing enough. But I had to find a way to get them away from each other.

'Sure,' I said. 'In that case we'll go in the lake. Shall we say out to the bridge and back?'

'You're crazy,' said Isaac. 'Are you serious?'

'Are you scared?'

'Don't take any notice of him,' said Kati. 'There's something the matter with him tonight. He said so himself.'

Isaac didn't take any notice of her. He was backed into a corner, too.

'Okay!' he said. 'But it's madness in this weather. And you don't stand a chance.'

'We'll see,' I said. 'If I win, you can leave Kati alone.'

Kati looked at me as if she didn't understand anything.

'Sure,' he said. 'And if I win you can shut up and go home.'

The others smiled. They pulled their jackets around them in the wind. I knew enough about parties to know that there is always a gossiping, shapeless lump of expectation that something, no matter what, should happen. Now something was about to happen.

They were pleased.

twelfth chapter

We are out of our depth, our strength runs out, we put something old over us and catch a glimpse of Paradise

It felt like putting your legs into a freezer. Slowly I transformed into a deep-frozen chicken with wrinkled, yellow-white skin, as I sank into the black water.

Isaac was a long way ahead of me. He had dived from the jetty in an elegant, well-trained arc. I get sore ears from diving, but that wouldn't have made any difference now. I looked like a loser right from the start when I crawled into the water, making a face, stepping out from the long curve of the beach.

'Give it up!' shouted Stefan when the water had just reached the top of my knickers. 'We'll call Isaac back again. It's childish.'

I knew he was right. But it didn't help. I pushed off in the direction I had seen Isaac's hair sticking up, at the same time a wave came crashing from the side so I almost couldn't see anything.

I wasn't a bad swimmer. Grandpa had taught me when I was little. And I had carried on swimming quite a lot, even since we stopped going to the island. Mum liked being able to look at water. Every summer we had always found some sea or a lake to splash around in. And I had spent quite a lot of time at the pool in wintertime.

But this was not a question of taking a summer swim in a warm tourist lake, where the sun glittered like marmalade on your breakfast toast. This was serious.

It might be seven or, at most, eight hundred metres to the bridge. But it felt like forever in the wind and the dark. Now and then I could glimpse the other side, shining rows of windows at the camping ground nearby, blinking between the waves.

I thought I had lost sight of Isaac. He had seemed to power away on the tops of the waves, as if this was one of his normal training sessions in the pool. But suddenly he appeared beside me. His hair was stuck around his head so I almost didn't recognize him. His face looked grey-blue in the gloom.

'Cold!' he sputtered.

'Yeah,' I said.

'Far enough, d'ya think?' he said.

Did he think I was going to give up? Or didn't he want to carry on? Maybe the cold had drained all his energy. Or was he suggesting some sort of truce? I didn't know. And I couldn't think in the searing cold.

I shook my head and fought to get past him.

'Lunatic!' he snorted.

He swam past me again kicking furiously, splashing me in the face. After a while he disappeared behind the white caps. I was alone.

I hadn't heard any voices from the beach for quite a while. And Isaac was gone. I was furious with myself. Why hadn't I answered him? Why hadn't I asked him what he meant? What was this absurd, stubborn pride that drove me on?

Suddenly I felt the cold pressing its way into me.

It hurt like thousands of needles in my skin. I couldn't feel my arms and legs. It was like when one of those injections starts to work and gradually you can't feel anything anymore. My body felt clumsy and heavy, and my swimming strokes stiff. How long could I carry on? I would have to try to get back again!

I turned and the waves came from the other side. I saw tall buildings glimmering in the distance. I aimed for them. All the time I was swallowing water and trying to cough it up. It felt harder and harder to go forwards, like swimming in a thick, ice-cold egg mixture which got stiffer the more you whisked around in it.

I want to live, I thought. I didn't want to sink into this awful, black, dead water which was hugging me with its strong arms so I couldn't get any air, holding me so hard against its beating breast that I couldn't move. My strength was starting to run out.

Then I heard a scream behind me.

It couldn't have been too far away. It must be Isaac!

I fought my way back, despair giving me strength. Water smashed me in the face. With all the effort, warmth and feeling started to return.

It wasn't long before I saw him. His head was bobbing like a buoy among the waves.

'I'm coming!' I screamed into the wind. 'Hang on, I'm coming!'

He was treading water and waved one arm so I could see where he was.

'I can't go any further!' he called. 'Help me! Please, help me!'

He looked really finished. Fear had transformed his face to a grimace that scared me. My God, what had I done? If he sank beneath those slapping waves it would be my fault! I only wanted him to like me. That's why I had tricked him out on this mad, fatal swimming tour!

'I don't know if I can,' I said.

I had reached him.

'You can't leave me!' he whimpered. 'Don't leave me!'

'I'm not going to! But keep calm, dammit. You're pulling us both down!'

I grabbed hold of his head and started to swim in the direction I thought the beach was in. I wasn't sure any more. Everything was quiet and dark and cold. I couldn't turn around and see if there were any lights. I felt his cold head against my chest.

'I'm sorry,' I said.

Maybe I was saying it to Isaac. Maybe to that lunatic God who was playing grim games with us. Maybe it was to Mum or Ingvar or Kilroy or anybody. I don't know.

Suddenly there were voices.

The clouds slid to one side and in a silver beam from the moon, I saw a rowing boat coming closer, wobbling over the waves.

'Here!' I screamed. 'Here we are!'

'What is it?' asked Isaac in a dull voice.

It seemed as if my scream had woken him up.

'They're coming,' I said. 'They're coming to get us!'

The light from a bobbing torch was searching for us.

'Here!' I called again. 'Can you see us?'

'There they are!' someone said at the same moment.

Isaac started to splash as if the anaesthetic in his body had worn off and some of his strength had returned.

'Let me go,' he said. 'I don't want them to see me like this. I can manage now, I'm sure.'

He held himself afloat. With stiff, flapping strokes he swam beside me while the boat rolled towards us with the splash of oars.

There were Fish and Dannie and Stefan and Pepsi, the whole of the terrible gang from the shed staring and grinning at us with wide eyes. They leaned over the edge with joyous cries so that the boat almost tipped over and they were close to falling in, like a big bunch of idiots.

'How are you doing?' screamed Fish. 'We borrowed a boat from a neighbour! We thought you'd be dead by now!'

'We'll pull you up from the stern,' called Stefan.

'Who said anything about being pulled up!' I yelled back. 'We're not tired. We're not finished yet!'

I was so pleased to see them that I felt completely warm. Who wanted to be pulled up like a crestfallen, trembling jellyfish? They would have to drag us into that rescue boat!

I carried on swimming and tried to look as athletic and well-rested as I could. And Isaac carried on valiantly at my side. I thought I saw a smile on his lips. It was the two of us! We played this deadly game together without giving up. Except now we knew they would never row away from us.

'Fantastic! I told you they could do it. Didn't I say so?' Danny said triumphantly. 'Isaac and Simon can do it, just like I said!'

'But you're going to have to get out of the water anyway,' said Fish, as if he was sorry for our sakes that he had to stop our little pleasure jaunt. 'The others are quite hysterical. They wanted to ring the police and the ambulance and sea rescue and I don't know what else when we left, the jitterbugs! So you'd better hop in before any of them start the world's biggest rescue mission!'

'That wouldn't be good, of course,' Isaac managed to say. 'We'll have to do this again another day!'

It wasn't easy to get us up into the boat. They were trampling on each other, hyped up and enthusiastic, and it was a miracle the boat didn't capsize. They dragged and pulled our arms till we finally landed in the bottom of the boat. As luck had it, they had brought a pile of blankets and towels Kati had given them. And our clothes were there as well. Except they were sopping wet after the clumsy rescue manoeuvre.

We wrapped ourselves in the towels and the blankets as best we could. Pepsi turned the boat around and rowed along Mångatan. A long way away, you could see Kati's house. When we came closer I saw black shadows moving in front of the windows. They were looking for us. I felt I didn't want to go back there. Ever. They would surround us and ask questions. I couldn't stand the thought. I wouldn't be able to act the part of being brave – a shivering, frozen hero with teeth chattering in time to the disco-drumming. I couldn't pretend for very much longer.

It didn't seem that Isaac was especially pleased with the idea of going back to the party either.

'Row us to the boatshed instead,' he said. 'Drop us off there first. Then we can go home from there. You can tell the others that Simon came first. He was way in front of me at the bridge. He was just waiting for me so we could come back together. Tell that to Kati.'

We looked at each other between the gaps in the tangled blankets.

I got cramp in my stomach. I got the hiccups from all the cold water I had swallowed.

We didn't go straight home. Neither of us had the energy. Our legs felt like the jelly snakes we'd been eating at the party. When the others had disappeared in the rowboat with shouts and happy farewells, the energy went out of us.

'We'll go into the boatshed and warm up a bit,' said Isaac. 'I'm so bloody cold. My stomach feels like a big lump of ice.'

'Mine too,' I said and managed to swallow a hiccup.

It was cold and damp inside. With fumbling fingers we managed to light anything that would warm us: the kerosene lamp, the Primus and the old woodstove in the corner. Slowly the woodstove heated up and the walls creaked as the sour cold was pushed out through the wood.

I was so tired I was almost crying. Everything we had wrapped around us had got wet during the boat trip and you could wring the water from our clothes which had been rolled up on the bottom of the boat. We would have to stay here a while.

We pulled off our blankets and towels and knickers. The heat from the stove's open door rushed towards us like a hot wind, and the fire cast fluttering shadows around the small room. I grabbed hold of the quilt from the bed to rub myself warm. It wasn't very clean, but it was at least dry.

Suddenly I could feel Isaac looking at me. I felt it as clearly as the heat from the stove. And I knew what he had seen! But I didn't care anymore. I was far too exhausted and cold and freezing to worry about giving myself away when I crawled out of those stuffed Olympia undies. It didn't matter anyway. Simon was gone now. He had drowned and wouldn't come up again. I turned towards Isaac. He looked groggy, as if he thought this was all too much for him, and he was somehow sick and seeing things that weren't there. Or that he wasn't seeing what should be there.

'I dropped it in the water,' I said, and giggled.

'You're crazy,' he said. 'Have you been a girl the whole time?'

Then he heard how stupid that sounded and he laughed too.

'My name is Simone,' I said.

Then we hung our clothes up on a string in front of the stove. We turned off the Primus stove. It had become really warm in the shed. The heat had the effect of a handful of sleeping tablets. Even if we'd wanted to, we wouldn't have been able to take ourselves out of there.

I had to lie down. I couldn't stand up any longer. And it was the same for him. Cautious and a bit embarrassed, he lay down beside me in the rickety bunk. It felt almost as unsafe as the rowing boat.

It felt strange to be lying there beside each other. His skin burned against mine.

'I almost can't believe this really,' he mumbled.

I stroked his hair which was starting to dry.

'Piss rat,' I whispered into the pillow.

'Baboon arse,' he replied, lightning fast.

'Skunk bum,' I laughed.

'Toad hole,' he laughed, putting his arm around me.

And I crept tight against him. I wanted to tell him that I liked him. But it would have to wait. I was scared I would hiccup in the middle of saying it. So we lay there waiting, and enjoyed all the waiting, while the stove snored in the corner, the kerosene lamp hummed softly and the walls creaked.

Soon it would be light.

thirteenth chapter

Some longed-for kisses are exchanged, I give up my Y-fronts, the Bun is dumbfounded and a wild beast waits for me on the steps

'I don't want to!' I complained.

He sat leaning over me with his freckled arms either side of my chest and his face close to mine.

'Don't be silly,' he said. 'Why not?'

'I just don't want to, that's all,' I said stubbornly.

The dawn light was filtered in through the window's irregular pattern of crushed flies and daddy-longlegs, and a drifting cloud of soot, dust and old smoke that coloured the wooden walls a romantic pink. Even Isaac looked pink.

'Please …' he pleaded.

'Not now,' I said. 'Not yet.'

No, I really didn't want to get up. I wasn't properly awake and it felt awful to meet the cold air. The stove had gone out. I wanted to carry on lying like before with my tummy against Isaac's back and our legs in a single tangle beneath the smelly old piece of cloth we had used as a quilt.

I grabbed hold of his tousled, blond mop and pulled him into bed again with the springs groaning and squeaking. He fell on his side and I pushed my nose into his armpit, like Kilroy used to do with me.

'I like you,' I said.

It was okay to say it like that. With my head right in that little hollow, like an ostrich. I didn't dare look at him.

'Stop it! That tickles like crazy!' He giggled and tossed and turned so the bad-smelling rag we had on top of us was swept onto the floor.

Then he lay still. His hand had landed on my stomach. It lay there quietly like a little naked animal. I stroked his skin gently, scared he would get up at any moment and leave me alone. During the night he had been a bit shocked by the cold water and tiredness. He hadn't had the chance to get used to the idea that I was a girl. Or else he was just trying to put a good face on things because I had kept his head above water for that moment before Pepsi and the others arrived with the boat. Was he grateful?

'You don't have to stay if you don't want to,' I said. 'I'm not going to make you.'

I held his arm tight.

'Let go of me then,' he said.

I snatched my hand away as if I had had an electric shock.

But he didn't disappear like I thought he would. He held my face with both hands and kissed me carefully, almost ceremoniously, on the end of my nose.

'Lunatic,' he said. 'I think I almost like you, too. Except it feels a little bit strange, everything.'

'For me too,' I said.

And then we kissed each other properly – but without tongues in each other's mouths, without biting and without Ulf Lundell's rasping voice in our ears. All that could be heard was the water washing the beach outside, some cheery morning birds chirping in the bushes and the blood drumming with impatience in my temples.

I lay with my head on his chest and looked down towards his toes. Between his feet his willy was standing up, like one of those party whistles you blew up with a squeak when you were little. It was bent in a funny little arch, like a big cheese doodle, coloured pink in the morning light.

'It's frozen!' I said and poked it a little. 'Look! It's all hard!'

He blushed and wriggled away.

'Dumb-bum,' he spluttered in a friendly way. 'Now we really do have to go. They'll be wondering what's happened to us.'

Yes, dammit! I hadn't thought of that.

We got dressed into our almost-dry clothes, locked the door to the shed and headed for home. We walked slowly, without saying anything, our arms crossed. My whole body hurt after yesterday's efforts. When you looked out over the lake, lightly touched by the morning breeze and glittering in the sunshine, it was hard to believe that just a few hours ago it had been a simmering and hissing death trap of angry, black, ice-cold water. It had transformed itself overnight and become something else, just like I had.

There wasn't a cloud in the sky. They had blown away like flapping demon's wings. It was still a bit cold. But it would be quite warm in a few hours.

Now warmth would finally return after the terrible spring. I could feel how the trees and plants were getting ready to put out their stalks and buds, unfolding their leaves like a jumble of green butterflies over the ground, and throwing out their flowers in white and yellow and blue. Even the stones on the beach looked as if they were full of life.

When we came to the hill towards the rubbish tip we went in different directions.

'See you at school then,' I said. 'I just have to get changed.'

It was well past eight when I biked back down the hill. My tyres sang and my chain rattled. Mum's old Northern Star bike was painted pink and white and gold. It matched my dress nicely.

It had taken me a long time to rummage in the wardrobe under the stairs. All my clothes were there, in a muddle. I hadn't had time to unpack properly since we moved. It hadn't felt especially tempting to sort out the dresses and skirts and blouses during my time as Simon. In the end, I decided on a pink dress with puffed sleeves and lace on the collar, and buttons like small plastic strawberries. Round my neck, I hung the gold heart Grandma and Grandpa gave me when I was born. This was also a kind of rebirth. On my feet I was wearing a pair of white Peter Pan boots. I had sprayed on a little of Mum's perfume, painted my lips a soft shade of pink that matched my dress and put mascara on my eyelashes.

That should do it. I almost didn't recognize myself when I looked in the mirror. I had got used to my boy-look; I had turned into that smirking, heavy-rock guy.

And now it felt as if I had climbed out again, this time into a girl. This girl with newly-washed hair, shining teeth and mascara-touched eyelashes looking at me in the mirror felt just as frightening, unreal and beautiful as the mannequins in Mum's magazines.

I had to calm down Mum and Ingvar as well. They had been a little concerned when I hadn't come home in the night. And it didn't get much better when I said that I had spent the night in an abandoned boatshed with a boy called Isaac.

All this took time.

When I swung into school, zigzagging past the ruminating ducks, and shoved my front wheel in the cycle stand, the others had long disappeared into the classroom.

Slowly and carefully, I opened the door.

Standing with her back to the door, the Bun didn't see me.

Anna was standing up at the front desk. In her left hand, she had a family-sized jam or apple sauce jar which held a collection of sticks. She had written THE WALKING STICK in big, childish letters on the blackboard. I had come in during the presentation of her cute little pets!

Anna continued to babble in her thin voice. She had a lot to do, balancing the heavy jar in one nervous hand, and with the other flicking through her papers where she had written down what she wanted to say. She wouldn't notice anything.

I didn't know what to do. Should I just go straight in and sit in my place (at least Simon's place) without saying anything? Or should I wait until someone who saw me got the teacher's attention? I couldn't decide.

I made a little wink at Isaac. And he made a face to show that he had seen me. The others mostly looked confused.

'Some walking sticks,' Anna carried on reading, 'or ghost insects as they are also known, can grow up to three metres long. Except mine are much shorter, of course. There are some that look like dried-up bits of grass while others look like stumps of broken branches and their long legs are like thin twigs. As further protection, many have stink glands which release caustic liquids …'

Those things in the jar were also pretending to be something other than what they were!

I saw from the Bun's back that she was shuddering at the thought of spidery stick stumps that could spray out stinking, caustic gunk at the drop of a hat.

I made a careful humming sound.

The Bun turned around and looked at me enquiringly.

'What do you want, then?' she said.

'It's me,' I said. 'It's just me.'

She stared as if I was one of those walking sticks, hard to place among all the other twigs and branches and sticks, and then her eyes lit up behind those glasses. She had recognized me!

'Simon!' she blurted.

'Yes,' I said. 'Or Simone, actually.'

'What?' she said.

'Simone,' I repeated. 'I'm not a boy. I'm a girl.'

The Bun looked absolutely helpless. Her face slowly reddened. The others didn't know what to think. They giggled a little uncertainly. They probably thought this was a new prank, a ploy, a joke.

'That's enough now.' Her voice was still reasonably composed. 'We have had enough pranks. Is that clear?'

This was going to be difficult.

'It's not a joke,' I said. 'I'm sorry, but I'm afraid it's true.'

'You can go home right now and put on your normal clothes and wipe that stuff off your face! I am starting to get tired of your constant fun-and-games.'

She had gone pale again; her face was turning a shade of greyish-yellow and her voice was getting harsher. 'Do you hear me, Simon?'

'Simone,' I corrected her.

Anna had picked her walking stick out of the jar and put it on her hand. It made its way slowly over the arm of her dress.

'Can I carry on now?' she asked.

'No!' screamed the Bun.

Anna wasn't used to anyone shouting at her. She jumped, and her beloved walking stick lost its footing and shot off though the emotionally-charged atmosphere to land on the back of Ant's hand. Ant was hardly prepared for that. Like everyone else, she was completely preoccupied with what was happening between the Bun and me. She jumped, too. That and her scream sent the walking stick crookedly over the row of desks till it landed somewhere in the Bun's complicated hairdo.

The Bun didn't make a sound. She went as stiff as a stick, herself. The walking stick looked like some kind of unique hairpin with those spiderlike twig legs stuck in her hair. At any moment it could spray the Bun's nest with its stink glands, that much was clear. The Bun looked as if she had a scorpion on her head.

Mum was afraid of spiders, but I had never been afraid of insects. I went up and carefully took the walking stick out of the Bun's hair. I put it back in the jar on the desk.

'I'm really sorry,' I said to the Bun. 'It seems to always end up like this, doesn't it? I can't control it. It just seems to happen, see? It's not anything I want. I'll leave now. Except actually it's true that I'm a girl.'

She looked so disturbed that I even went up and patted her on the cheek.

'Don't be angry with me,' I added. 'It will all get better, you'll see.'

I almost felt like an adult comforting a child.

'I can confirm that she's a girl,' Isaac said suddenly in a high voice.

Everyone turned and looked at him. He went bright red in the face, as if he had said too much.

'A girl!' Kati groaned indignantly. 'And that's what I've been in love with!'

Even the Bun smiled then.

'Goodbye,' she said as I went out through the door.

I was so tired that the bike wobbled when I swung into the gravel path up to the house. The hill had almost done me in. I hadn't had very many hours sleep that night. I felt as if I hadn't slept for at least a week. But now everything would quieten down a bit. Now I would be a good and quiet girl whom no one noticed and everyone left alone, and the only unusual thing about me would be my unusual name, Simone. I would be able to sit and relax in class and answer almost all the questions correctly and never be accused of cheating or being rowdy or bad. The smoking and the bad boatshed gang would have to go. Now and then, I could go with Isaac to some Flashdance film and hold his hand in the dark and taste his cool lips.

But no, it wasn't going to be like that!

A loud *grrraaaaoouup!* sounded from near my feet as I almost tripped on the big and hairy thing stretched across the steps. Then it landed on me, a dreadlocked, smelly, dirty monster whose powerful paws on my chest tumbled me backwards into the bumblebee-humming flowerbed. It stuck its stinking mouth over my face and dragged its coarse tongue like a sponge over my eyelids, mascara and lipstick before it turned around and whacked me on the ear with its shabby tail.

'Kilroy!' I yelled. 'Is it really you, you old bag of rubbish! What have you been eating? You stink!'

He didn't answer. I almost couldn't believe it. How had he survived for over a week? Where had he found food? Where had he been sleeping during these cold, wet, terrible nights? But, in any case, it was him, even though there wasn't much left of his snow-white, shining, light-pawed elegance.

I rolled around with him on the lawn and pushed my hands into his coarse, filthy coat. And he yelped and barked and wagged his tail from happiness and pride in having smelt his way to our house in the middle of nowhere.

Then we stormed inside.

'Mum, Ingvar, Grandpa! Kilroy's come back!' I shouted.

Everyone gathered around Kilroy. We felt his legs and his stomach and his back to see if anything was wrong. We tried to look inside his mouth to see if it was swollen. But we couldn't find any faults other than a scratch in his left ear.

'Have you been in a fight, you terrible beast?' I said.

'Aaaawwwoooo!' he whimpered, ashamed.

'He could do with a bath. He doesn't smell very good,' Ingvar said.

I took him down to the bathtub and shampooed and rinsed and dried him. I brushed his coat till it got back its old shine, and he was brimming with wellbeing.

When he had eaten the meat we were going to have for dinner, a few sausages, some liver paté, salami, and half a litre of pistachio ice cream with chocolate sauce, he burped and blinked sleepily. He gave a big yawn. He was probably just as tired as I was.

I made a bed for us both in the mahogany monster. And while I could hear Grandpa rolling around in his wheelchair in the kitchen, calling instructions to Mum and Ingvar about various dishes, telephoning people and inviting guests to the party he was having the next day, Kilroy and I lay and chatted and got each other up-to-date about everything that had happened since last we saw each other.

I slept with my nose in his warm, soft coat. Even in my sleep I could hear Grandpa's singing voice.

fourteenth chapter

The chandelier hangs in the apple tree, the old people's orchestra plays, Grandpa and I rub noses for the last time, and the party and life continues into the night

I slept. I slept the whole afternoon. I got woken up towards the evening so I could eat something. We ate in the kitchen. It was a big mess of jugs, platters, pots, frying pans and bowls, and the air was full of steam and a thousand smells. Then I went to sleep again, to the sound of pots and wooden spoons and whisking.

I didn't wake again until the moon was shining in through the window and Grandpa was leaning over my bed with his shiny, bald head like another moon. I don't know if he touched me or not. Maybe I just woke with him sitting and looking at me.

When I opened my eyes he placed his gigantic hand in mine.

'I just thought I would sit here for a while,' he said. 'Before I go to bed.'

I nodded. It felt like when I was small and had the measles and got so sick that no one knew how it would end. Then Grandpa had sat like this at my bed with his hand in mine. But now I didn't feel especially sick. In fact, I was feeling a lot better than I had in ages.

'Does it feel better now?' Grandpa asked.

It was as if he could hear what I was thinking.

'Mmm,' I said.

And so I told him, giggling, about what had happened since our last night talk. It was so easy to talk in the dark, without a whole lot of confusing stuff around. I told him about the ducks and the party at Kati's, about the fight with the cold and the waves in the sea, about Isaac and the boatshed, and the Bun's disbelieving face when I revealed my secret. And his hand over mine felt heavy like a sun-warmed stone and yet still light, as if it was still stroking the smashed cello.

'It seems as if the demons have left you for a bit,' he said, 'which might feel a little empty. Even though it sounds crazy, you can actually miss the things you don't like when they've disappeared. Isn't that strange?' He sighed.

And I felt that he meant more than he was saying.

'Yeah,' I said.

Then it was quiet. Kilroy snuffled and the clocks ticked.

'Well, I probably should go up and sleep now, little crow,' he said.

But he didn't go.

He stayed sitting and placed his hand in mine, to make it look as if I was the one stopping him from going. 'Do you remember …' he said.

And we remembered together as the hours passed. It was cool in the woods of childhood, in the blueberry scrub or by the raspberry bushes; the adders stuck up their waving heads, but there was no danger; and the suns of the past shone on us and dried us after the rains and swims. We let our memories flow together, making a shaft of sunlight in the dark.

'Isn't it time for you to come to bed, Father?' Mum called from upstairs.

'Soon!' he called back.

But he didn't go.

He sat there.

'You see, my dear nincompoop,' he said slowly. 'Tomorrow I have invited my friends here. I want to say goodbye, you see. And now I feel it's time.'

The stormy black water from yesterday hurled itself through the gap in the window, and washed over me, ice cold and pitiless. That's how it felt. I grabbed Grandpa's hand. I knew what he meant.

'It's not true,' I whispered. 'You're lying! You can't die.'

But I knew that he wasn't lying. He didn't need to lie.

'Don't be sad, my darling child,' he said quietly. 'I'm old. My body is tired and it can't go on. And then, of course, I'm a little bit curious about what's going to come next. For the dipsticks the thing is quite settled – either eternal sleep or eternal life. But for us fruitloops, it must be something unclear. If everything was done and dusted then there wouldn't be any fruitloops. And if there was a God then it would be a dipstick sort of God and quite dull. And in that case it would be better to have eternal sleep. God save me from eternal life as a dipstick!'

I knew he was smiling his crooked wolf smile in the dark.

He stayed beside me in the quiet, until sorrow stilled to melancholy and melancholy changed to tiredness when the first light of dawn found its way into the room.

Then he went off with heavy steps up the stairs. Maybe he thought I was asleep.

I searched for the crystal ball that I hadn't looked in for ages. I don't know what I expected to see. The fruitloops' heaven with Grandpa as a smiling saint? When I looked into it, the light condensed to a glowing point. And then I saw Grandpa in the garden, surrounded by birds and butterflies and people.

'And then?' I whispered impatiently, and knocked the cool glass egg with my knuckles.

With a sharp clink, that solid crystal ball split into two. I held its lifeless halves between my hands.

The afternoon sun shone between woolly clouds.

The guests started to arrive at around six o'clock. Some came by taxi, others by bus and then there were some who looked as tired and worn out as if they had walked all the way to our garden.

Grandpa had been busy the whole day. He had driven around in his wheelchair putting final touches to the food and decorations. He looked ruddy-cheeked and healthy, and he hummed enthusiastically, a little off-key. Was it just a mask, a way of holding worry at bay? Or was he wrong?

As the guests arrived, Grandpa received each of them with a heartfelt greeting and loud kisses on their cheeks. He lay, or half-lay to be more precise, in the mahogany monster we had carried out to the garden beneath the flowering cherry tree, with a collection of cushions at his back like billowing summer clouds dragged straight down from the sky.

I didn't recognize most of the people who came. Many were probably from the hospital: trembling old men and women with walking sticks and crutches and smiling faces, well-dressed in dark suits and shiny dresses. The garden was filled with the fragrance of hairspray and heavy perfumes.

I stood beside Grandpa's bed, wearing the flowery silk dress that once belonged to Grandma, that he had given me on the island.

'This is Simone, my favourite fruitloop,' Grandpa said, introducing me.

'My poor girl,' said a lady in a black straw hat and she hugged me with her skinny arms. Her whole body was shaking.

Mum went around in Grandma's old Parisian hat, serving punch that Grandpa had made in the ether-green tub. It looked like a bathtub for grapes, kiwifruit, slices of lemon and white flower petals.

'Now, dear friends,' Grandpa called in his singing voice. 'Now you must start eating, and consider yourselves warmly welcome, all you dear curlicues!'

We sat at the long table with its white tablecloth wafting gently in the light breeze. Any stiffness quickly disappeared. The table overflowed with patés and pirogues, many kinds of pickled herrings, herb-crusted chicken legs, and duck breast covered in pressed-raspberry sauce. It was all washed down with lemon water, wine and Berlin cocktails.

Grandpa didn't eat much himself. He just tried a forkful of everything.

I wanted to make him a plate, but he shook his head. 'Today I just want to enjoy watching others eat,' he said. 'I'm not really hungry.'

I wasn't either. But the others helped themselves enthusiastically from plates of food, salad and fruit.

Their voices rose, and the ringing laughter rose to the tops of the trees while the sun balanced like a ripe peach on the peak of the rubbish tip.

'I love you all!' called Grandpa and raised his glass.

Twilight came slowly, and the orchestra started to play. It was the orchestra Grandpa had started at the old people's home. But today he just wanted to hear the others play. The violins squeaked like crickets, the clarinet hummed high as a tomcat, the drums banged, the accordion bleated like a choir of sheep. The lady in the black straw hat played a harp as if she was combing and combing a mane of hair. And dancers swirled between the trees.

In the apple tree, Ingvar had hung up the chandelier. He had climbed the tree in his plaster cast, without even falling down. High in the greenery, the candles burned with swaying flames. And on the lawn where people weren't dancing, the outside candles shone above the hoops in the croquet lawn, so people could see where they were hitting. Two old men were arguing loudly about whether one had hit the stick or not.

'I'll hit you in the head, you old nut!' One of them threatened the other with his croquet club.

He happened to hit Axelsson, who had arrived to complain about the noise, so that he tumbled back into his already severely damaged hedge. But Mum lifted him out again and danced with his head resting on her cleavage till he smiled like a comforted child.

Grandpa sat in his bed like a smiling God leaning against his clouds. He drummed his fingers against the bed, in time to the music, and sipped his cup of tea, with the samovar hissing beside him.

'Let the party carry on,' whispered Grandpa.

He held my hand and Mum's between his. The moon splashed its glitter over us. He closed his eyes and lay his head on the pillows. We didn't say anything. We stood there with our hands in his while his breaths became weaker and finally disappeared.

I bent down slowly over Grandpa's face and rubbed my nose against his, just like we did when I was a little whippersnapper and he was the good and wise God. His moustache tickled and I thought he was smiling at me.

And life and the party carried on into the night.